W9-ABN-313

Coming of Age as a Poet

Helen Vendler

Coming of Age
as a Poet

MILTON

KEATS

ELIOT

PLATH

Harvard University Press

Cambridge, Massachusetts

London, England

2003

Page 169 constitutes an extension of the copyright page.

Library of Congress Cataloging-in-Publication Data

Vendler, Helen Hennessy.
Coming of age as a poet : Milton, Keats, Eliot, Plath / Helen Vendler.
p. cm.
Includes bibliographical references and index.
Contents: John Milton : the Elements of Happiness—John Keats : Perfecting the Sonnet—
T. S. Eliot : Inventing Prufrock—Sylvia Plath : Reconstructing the Colossus.
ISBN 0-674-01024-8 (alk. paper)
1. English poetry—History and criticism.
2. American poetry—20th century—History and criticism.
3. Eliot, T. S. (Thomas Stearns), 1888–1965—Criticism and interpretation.
4. Milton, John, 1608–1674—Criticism and interpretation.
5. Keats, John, 1795–1821—Criticism and interpretation.
6. Plath, Sylvia—Criticism and interpretation.
7. Maturation (Psychology) in literature. I. Title.
PR502.V46 2003   2002027287
820.9—dc21

For George and Joanna, generous friends

ACKNOWLEDGMENTS

Three of the four chapters of *Coming of Age as a Poet* were originally delivered as the James Murray Brown Lectures at the University of Aberdeen. I am grateful to Professor George Watson, who invited me to Aberdeen, and to his wife, Joanna, for their exceptional hospitality and friendship during my stay; to Duncan Rice, Principal, and Graeme Roberts, Dean, whose kindness of welcome I have felt on more than one occasion; to Professor Tom Devine, for a generous introduction to the work of his Research Institute of Irish and Scottish Studies; and to my friend Marian Connor, who lent me her company in Aberdeen. Professor Lawrence Buell, of the Harvard University English Department, and President Neil Rudenstine of Harvard granted me a semester's half-time leave for medical reasons while I was composing this book; in a time of discouragement, their solicitude brought solace. My thanks to Professor Ruth Stevenson of Union College, who read part of this book in draft and made helpful comments; and to my incomparable editor Margaretta Fulton of Harvard University Press, who urged me to turn the Aberdeen lectures into a book, who suggested additions after reading the first draft, who answered questions, and who was, as always, patient with my delays.

Contents

AUTHOR'S NOTE

I have kept documentation to a minimum in this book: a full citing of critical commentary on such well-known poems would overwhelm these brief essays. I have used a grave accent to mark sounded "ed," to alert the modern reader to the correct pronunciation (so important for rhythm) of words where it occurs in Milton and Keats. In making statements on "the poet," I will use "he" in general remarks and in the chapters on Milton, Keats, and Eliot, and "she" in the chapter on Plath; but I intend my general remarks to apply to both sexes.

Coming of Age as a Poet

Introduction

I N EACH of the four essays in this book, I consider the work a young poet has to have done before writing his or her first "perfect" poem—the poem which first wholly succeeds in embodying a coherent personal style. To the young writer, the search for a style is inexpressibly urgent; it parallels, on the aesthetic plane, the individual's psychological search for identity—that is, for an authentic selfhood and a fitting means for its unfolding. The human search for identity is conducted blindly; we find ourselves as adolescents suffering an incomprehensible series of apparently random preferences, revulsions, divagations, and evasions. We don't at the time know why our feelings drift hither and yon on the waves of inexplicable compulsions, griefs, and admirations: it is only later that we may be prepared to acknowledge, with Wordsworth, how strange are the ways of identity-formation:

> How strange that all
> The terrors, pains, and early miseries,
> Regrets, vexations, lassitudes, interfused
> Within my mind, should e'er have borne a part,
> And that a needful part, in making up
> The calm existence that is mine when I
> Am worthy of myself!
> (1850 *Prelude,* I, 344–350)

Wordsworth awakes after early miseries, regrets, and terrors to an adult identity, pursuing an existence which derives calm from its conscious awareness of its selfhood, no longer mystified by youth's emotional vicissitudes.

Wordsworth has recounted in this passage the normal course of individual human formation. But for a young writer, the stakes are doubled. The youthful writer cannot pursue an evolution to adulthood independent of an ongoing evolution of style. To find a personal style *is*, for a writer, to become adult. Much in the formation of style takes place relatively unconsciously: in both random and directed reading, the young poet is insensibly drawn to some predecessors, finds others uninteresting, is unaware as yet of ones soon to be discovered, rejects others as unappealing. But the ultimate style of a poet is also partly chosen (often in rebellion against available discourses): to write about landscape rather than about persons; to resort to mythology or not; to operate within a close logical format or to range more intuitively; to approach or veer away from the demotic; to write personally or impersonally; to settle on certain forms or stanzas that will become habitual.

We will be seeing four young writers in search of a style: John Milton, John Keats, T. S. Eliot, and Sylvia Plath. In considering the first "perfect" poem each of these poets writes, I count as "perfect" the poem in which, with confidence, mastery, and above all ease, each comes of age as a poet to be reckoned with. I call such poems "perfect" because they manifest a coherent and well-managed idiosyncratic style voiced in memorable lines; one would not wish them other than they are. Such a poem is one that a reader will recognize as "Miltonic" or "Keatsian": that is, the style is visibly continuous, at least in part, with that of the poet's later work. It is a poem that will become canonical within the poet's oeuvre: its imaginative powers are so characteristic and deep, and its technique so matches them in ambition, that an anthologist or teacher is likely to choose it when illustrating the early work of the author, and younger poets will tend to raid it for their own purposes—which may range from imitation to parody, but which reflect creative incorporation. My four chosen poems—*L'Allegro, On First Looking into Chapman's Homer, The Love Song of J. Alfred Prufrock,* and *The Colossus*—though composed in their authors' youth, have exhibited literary staying power. (I will sometimes set these early "perfect" efforts against less accomplished or even embarrassing preceding poems, or against more "advanced" later poems, to sharpen our sense of the poet's discoveries in the search for an adult style.)

I have taken up this subject in part because it's popularly believed that anything written in unjustified lines is reasonably called a poem. In the broadest sense—that which distinguishes verse from prose—it is. But to earn the label "poem" in its fullest sense, the piece of verse must be almost superhumanly accomplished. It is the product of a writer who—no matter how young—has gone through an intense (and successful) self-apprenticeship in poetry. It is this fact that Emerson took for granted when, in responding to Whitman's gift of *Leaves of Grass,* he surmised that the fully-achieved poems in that volume were the result of a "long foreground." (The accuracy of Emerson's intuition can be confirmed by a glance at the young Whitman's prose and verse prior to *Leaves of Grass.*) The long foreground of composition preceding an author's best early work is often amply available (as it is in the case of Keats and Eliot and Plath). Sometimes it is largely missing. We know, for instance, that Milton practiced his art for some years before writing even the earliest of the extant poems. Before Milton was twelve, he was exchanging Latin and Greek verses with his tutor; and at St. Paul's School—before leaving at sixteen—he composed, according to his brother Christopher, "many Copies of Verses: which might well become a riper age."[1] All of these verses are lost.

Since the record of apprenticeship is often overlooked by readers who encounter only the poet's successful poems in anthologies or selected editions, the indispensable process of exploratory learning and experiment can vanish from view. And without school training in poetry, new readers often find it difficult to distinguish an imaginatively and linguistically striking poem from ineptly-divided prose masquerading as free verse. I hope to show here, with respect to a few youthful compositions (all written while the authors were still in their twenties), the private, intense, and ultimately heroic effort and endurance that precede the creation of any memorable poem. The solitary work of living the life of the composing artist—its patience under inner tension, its belief in its own necessity—has been tersely described by Emily Dickinson:

> Each – its difficult idea
> Must achieve – Itself –
> Through the solitary prowess
> Of a Silent Life –
>
> Effort – is the sole condition –
> Patience of Itself –
> Patience of opposing forces –
> And intact Belief –
>
> Looking on – is the Department
> Of its Audience –
> But Transaction – is assisted
> By no Countenance –[2]

Audience and Countenance come later, and have given the poems here their fame. But the difficult idea and the solitary prowess in the quiet room came first.

What sorts of discoveries in style does the youthful poet need to make? A governing stylistic decorum needs to be acquired (down to the smallest details of technique); this consciousness of the lyric medium is accompanied psychologically by a growing awareness of the problems attending accurate expression of inner moods and attitudes. The poet needs also to identify the salient elements of the outer sense-world that speak to his idiosyncratic imagination; to devise his own particular axes of time and space; to decide on the living and non-living beings who will populate his work; and finally to find a convincing cosmological or metaphysical frame of being within which the activity of the poem can occur. Let me say a little more about each of these stylistic experiments.

First of all, there are, as I have said, the intuitive technical discoveries made in the course of early experimentation. The young poet advances on many fronts at once (often shakily), learning how to manage sound (the sounds of syllables, words, phrases, and lines); rhythm (iambs and trochees, tetrameters and pentameters, caesuras and line-breaks, intonation and phrasing); syntax (including individually distinctive sentence-forms); and larger formal units such as stanzas and sonnets.[3] In order to make the voice that emerges sound like an individual self (yet a self that can and does change, even minute by minute, in psychological response), the young poet will work intensely at technique—changing, improving, varying those things already learned, investigating new paths. Until some of these technical skills begin to come (after much repetition) into play by instinct, the young poet has no chance of writing a perfect poem. A poet also needs to learn to manage consistency and plausibility of stylistic motivation: a poem can't veer uncontrollably from attitude to attitude, tone to tone. It must discover a fit governance of its evolving material, to practice that stylistic decorum which, as Milton said in *Of Education,* "is the great masterpiece to observe."[4]

Along with experimentation in the elements of language, the poet has to identify, and find words for, the salient presences constituting the geographical and historical elements of the physical universe as it is to be selectively recreated in his poetry—as, for instance, Wordsworth discovered (geographically speaking) mountains and cottages and (historically speaking) the French Revolution and the Terror as elements constituting his inner world. As we know, Milton, who was to be an encyclopedic poet, would eventually choose to include in his recreated world almost everything found in mythical and geographical space and in theological and historical time. Such unbounded inclusiveness is far from necessary to a poet of intimate colloquy such as George Herbert; but Milton had to find a way to mirror, in what he wrote, the vast reach of his characteristic sense of the world. The thrashing about that young poets do until they find the contextual materials and *dramatis personae* that match their sensibility is often both comic and painful to observe, and even more painful, of course, to endure. On the other hand, when they come upon the particulars they need, they are elated: Eliot's excitement when he found exactly the material sordidness he needed in the grim urban scenes of Baudelaire is palpable in his essays and letters.

In developing an individual style, young writers have not only to invent a selective verbal simulacrum of the outer world; they have also to find a coordinate set of symbolic equivalents for their central psychological dilemmas. As we know, for Milton tensions accrue between temptation and virtue; for Keats, between sensual receptivity and a strenuous will to "philosophize"; for Eliot, between sardonic irony and spiritual aspiration; for Plath, between "femininity" and a drive to power. The first "perfect" poem may show only one half of such contendings within the person; nonetheless, what it reveals will be authentic, and will be continuous with at least some of what is to follow.

So far, I have been writing as though the poet were concerned only with expressing a single sense of the outer world and the inner self. But there is also, usually, some larger community demanding a voice in his poetry. Even if the young writer is a lyric poet rather than an epic or narrative one, he must also adopt a social stance, a position vis-à-vis other people. This stance can be one of exclusion (under ethical norms, as in Milton) or one of inclusion (as in Keats's extensions of friendship); or one of observant but chilly fascination (as in Eliot); or one of domestic denunciation (as in Plath). Who is to live in the young poet's social world? Sometimes it can seem as though that world is populated only by blood relatives (as in Lowell's *Life Studies*) or by God (as in Herbert's *The Temple*). Deciding on the living inhabitants of one's imaginative work, and one's relations with those inhabitants, is one of the necessities facing young poets. Writers can often be initially mistaken about the population they are psychologically suited to describe: Milton thought of writing his epic about the personages of English history, but discovered that his imagination responded more deeply to those of biblical narrative. While absorbed in pastoral, Keats wrote—even before understanding the full cost—of the necessary passage from the coupled solitude of the erotic to the tragedy of the social whole:

> . . . In the bosom of a leafy world
> We rest in silence, like two gems upcurled
> In the recesses of a pearly shell.
>
> And can I ever bid these joys farewell?
> Yes, I must pass them for a nobler life,
> Where I may find the agonies, the strife
> Of human hearts. . . .
> (*Sleep and Poetry*, 119–124)

However, Keats was not able to put this 1816 prediction into practice until 1818, when he transferred his literary allegiance from Spenser to Shakespeare. Plath, before her death, had directed her gaze outward from the solitary lyric self only as far as the family constellation—but in her metaphors for that family (from the Atlantic cable to the Holocaust) she had begun to cast a wider social net.

Finally—to conclude this minimal list of ever-broadening things to be learned and invented—the young poet must imagine, and find a style for, a world-cosmology that goes beyond earthly elements, inner tensions, and social relations. Milton is famous for his inventions in this respect; but even a poet so bound to the domestic as Plath must extend herself out to a governing moon, or to such lines as "fixed stars govern a life." Keats, for his part, must reach to describe, even if to repudiate, the constancy of the North Star, and must realize, through what he called "the sacred seasons," the inevitability of process and death; Eliot looks toward the still point of the turning world, presided over by the dove descending.

This list of stylistic paths to an adult poetic identity could be extended, but I've said enough to remind readers of how much technical work, introspection, and imaginative reflection must precede any signal accomplishment in poetry. Of course, the "perfect" first poem may be seen as something partial when we review it with hindsight after our acquaintance with the later work of the writer. Yet I want often to forgo hindsight here, and to move only as far as each of the young poets has moved. I want to see what they saw, in their youth, when they managed to rise, in a page or two, to imaginative power and aesthetic ease. They naturally then go on to acquire further purposings: we can see those ampler ambitions in Milton as he proceeds from *L'Allegro* to *Il Penseroso,* including in the second poem visions of learning and prophetic age that are absent from *L'Allegro.* We can see a comparable larger desire arising in other poets: in Keats as he prepares to pass from sonnets to his first long poem, *Endymion;* or in Eliot's conceiving, after his Prufrockian duo, "you and I," the variously populated scenes of *The Waste Land;* and in Plath's merciless critiques-by-revision of the gentility of her own early work. All four of our poets continued to change after writing their first "perfect" poem. But we halt with them here as each achieves, for an extraordinary moment, what Stevens calls (in *A Primitive Like an Orb*) "the rightness that pulls tight the final ring."

In rehearsing, for the new reader, familiar facts and opinions about these well-known poems, I have needed to present information already well known to scholars. But I hope in each case to have added something new to our perception of the poems I've treated.

I have said nothing in this Introduction about the poet's finding a "theme"—the abstraction, or concept, or message, that will press voice into impassioned speech. The importance of a theme is not to be doubted; and in the essays that follow I will be saying something about the force, in each case, of the concepts generating the chosen poem. But themes change over a poet's lifetime. What never changes is the poet's need in *every* poem—no matter what its theme—for decorum, for an imagined symbolic equivalent to the stress of feeling, for a matching and original technique, for salient earth-elements placed in axes of time and space, for social relations (or a refusal thereof), and for a metaphysics or cosmology implied in the activity of the poem. Any "perfect poem" will have to exhibit a believable mastery of these elements: without them, its theme would be inert, its message forgettable. Both we as readers, and poets as writers, participate in the necessary belief that it is the urgent theme that drives the writer. So it does—but it is the writing that gives the theme life. How it does so, in these perfect youthful constellations of words, is the matter of the chapters that follow.

1

JOHN MILTON

The Elements of Happiness

I T IS PRECISELY because *L'Allegro* and *Il Penseroso* have always been treated together that I want to separate them. Cleanth Brooks goes so far as to call them a "double poem," and later refers to the two together as "the poem":[1] whatever they are, they are not that. They are visibly two separate poems as printed in 1645, and it muddies the critical waters, when considering *L'Allegro,* always to see it merely as a stepping-stone to *Il Penseroso. Il Penseroso* indeed reveals an ambition in Milton to arrive ultimately at full philosophical knowledge, to live "Till old experience do attain / To something like prophetic strain." But when he wrote these companion poems, Milton was, after all, in his twenties—1631, his twenty-fourth year, is the generally accepted date—and in *L'Allegro* we find the young Milton at the actual time of writing, not as he hopes to be in his sixties. *L'Allegro* is the poem of his "now," the poem in which he finds his present happiness. It is also the poem in which he first shows ease in extending a poem in time and space, and since extension will be his major quality as a poet, it is worth noting when and how he first does it right. Even if the poems were conceived as a pair, in the passion for dialectic that Milton was never to lose, I count *L'Allegro* as Milton's first triumph, and intend to consider it as my example of his first "perfect" poem. But I must postpone this central topic while I weigh the claims of the work that many have cited as Milton's first masterpiece—*On the Morning of Christ's Nativity,* often referred to as the Nativity Ode.[2]

In that poem, written before *L'Allegro,* Milton had certainly attempted a far grander extension than those we see in the paired poems. The Nativity Ode is in this sense the most "Miltonic" of Milton's early poems, but it is not a poem without difficulties of execution. I would not want to call those difficulties blemishes, exactly, but the poem does not exhibit the effortless ease of *L'Allegro.*[3] The Nativity Ode aims at more, but strains at its ambitions. In it, Milton covers all of recorded time, whether conceived in classical terms (from the Golden Age to the fallen present) or Judeo-Christian ones (from the creation of the angels to "the world's last session"). He also ranges through all of space, from the heaven where angels sing to the earth where shepherds sit, down to the realm of "the old dragon underground." In the Nativity Ode he identifies one of his fundamental oppositions—that between the pagan and the Judeo-Christian ideas of divinity. The author of the Nativity Ode—like the protagonist of *Il Penseroso*—is the Milton we will eventually come to know, in his full powers, in *Paradise Lost*. And we are moved when we see how soon Milton's imaginative ambitions stretched to include all of time and all of space—even if those ambitions were not to be fully realized in adequate form for decades.

Yet the Nativity Ode, however impressive, is, I believe, too small a container, aesthetically speaking, for the epic history—divine, angelic, diabolic, and human; theological, allegorical, mythological, and literal—that it attempts to encompass. Its narrative contents are disproportionate to its scale; they would require an epic length to display them without awkwardness. The awkwardness I mention doesn't arise immediately: the proem and the first eleven stanzas of the poem proper ("The Hymn" that follows the proem), which track closely the events of the Nativity narrative, are confident and gracious. It is winter; God has sent a universal peace; in the night "the Prince of light" begins his reign; the stars stand fixed, and the sun delays his "inferior flame" now that a greater Sun has appeared; the shepherds are addressed by the angels' music. At stanza XII, however, Milton departs from this chronological narrative to begin a characteristic Miltonic extension of time: after veering back to the creation of the world, he entreats the spheres to ring out their music so that "Time will run back, and fetch the age of gold," ushering in a new age of truth and justice and mercy, when heaven will open the gates of her "Palace Hall." This wide temporal sweep—back to the beginning of Creation and the Golden Age, and forward to a new Golden Age to come—is checked at the beginning of stanza XVI with a brief rebuke, which serves as preface to a specimen of Miltonic time-compression and time-leaping. This section is what I and others find awkward; its hasty brevity is out of proportion to the long Nativity narrative and to the relatively ample circuit of Creation and the future Golden Age:

> Heav'n . . .
> Will open wide the Gates of her high Palace Hall.

>   XVI
> But wisest Fate sayes no,
> This must not yet be so,
>   The Babe lies yet in smiling Infancy,
> That on the bitter cross
> Must redeem our loss;
>   So both himself and us to glorifie;
> Yet first to those ychain'd in sleep,
> The wakefull trump of doom must thunder through
>   the deep.

The time-scheme of these ten lines (the last two of stanza XV and the eight lines of XVI) takes us on the following journey:

(1) At the end of the world we shall see righteousness return;
(2) But not yet (says Fate);
(3) The Babe is new-born now;
(4) He must grow up and die on the cross;
(5) So to glorify himself and us (on the last day);
(6) But first the dead must wake to the last trump.

We have (twice in ten lines) scanned the time from now to the end of the world, and have seen (within two lines) Jesus born and crucified; we have then jumped forward to the glorification of the just, but afterward leapt back to the last trump.

By contrast to the confining of most of time in this cramped ten-line procrustean bed, the poet's treatment of space in the Nativity Ode is luxurious. He allows himself forty-eight lines (stanzas XIX to XXIV) to move from Delphi to Palestine to Persia to Libya to Tyre to Egypt, as one by one the classical deities are unmanned by the presence of the Babe, who "Can in his swadling bands control the damnèd crew." Finally, in a two-stanza coda, as dawn arrives and the last pagan spirits fade, the narrator concludes:

> But see the Virgin blest
> Hath laid her Babe to rest.
>   Time is our tedious Song should here have ending:
> Heav'ns youngest teemèd Star,
> Hath fixt her polisht Car,
>   Her sleeping Lord with Handmaid Lamp
>   attending:
> And all about the Courtly Stable,
> Bright-harnest Angels sit in order serviceable.

This beautifully still tableau—the Virgin, the sleeping child, the fixed star, and the seated Angels—"corrects" the "mistake" in the proem, in which the Son of God is said to have laid aside his heavenly form: he

> here with us to be,
>   Forsook the Courts of everlasting Day
> And chose with us a darksom House of mortal Clay.

We see at the conclusion of the poem that the Savior did not "forsake" the Courts of everlasting Day: where he is, they are. Where he is, in the paradoxically "Courtly" stable, the bright-harnessed Angels attend on him, ready for service. This ending is one of the many brilliant moments in the poem; and we can recall, in praising aspects of the poem, how Keats was moved to borrow, for his own odes, certain of its telling details (the "pale-mouth'd prophet" of the *Ode to Psyche*; the "Queen-Moon" of the *Ode to a Nightingale* surrounded by her "starry Fays").

Yet there is, it seems to me, a fundamentally ungainly disproportion in the disposition of the materials of time and space in the Nativity Ode, as a lofty young imagination tries to achieve its desired effect—that of epic breadth—in a lyric form of too brief a scope for its ambitions. The Ode has neither the structural mastery nor the rhythmic ease that we find in *L'Allegro*.[4] And it is achievement—not ambition of intent, nor thematic prophecy of a future career—that is my concern here. Conceding the undeniable beauties of the Ode, I nonetheless turn, for my example of "perfection," to the graceful, beautiful, and unerring *L'Allegro*.

In *L'Allegro* we see the youthful Milton wholly accomplishing, with intellectual success and aesthetic confidence, the task he has set for himself: to see which "unreprovèd pleasures" might be allowed to human beings. He invents a single protagonist (a cultivated person) and, parallel to him, a collective protagonist (a group of rustics). The separately-lived lives of the two protagonists are tracked through a single multiseasonal "day" from dawn to late night. These lives are arranged chiastically: we see the educated protagonist's day; then the rustics' day and the rustics' night; then the educated protagonist's night. I will have more to say about this arrangement.

Milton's powerful senses demanded that he explore the scope of their pleasures; his even more powerful ethical instinct demanded that he explore all pleasures, of body and of spirit, in a manner consistent with his principles. What is licit? What may be experienced or done? What may one enjoy without criticism from self or others? What are the sources of happiness? These are certainly the thematic questions of the poem; but they are not questions original to Milton. (The question of the respective merits of the active and the contemplative life raised by *L'Allegro* and *Il Penseroso* was old by Milton's time; such topics were often assigned as academic exercises.) It is what Milton does with his conventional themes that will interest us.

Commentators on *L'Allegro,* as the Milton *Variorum* reveals, have tended, on the one hand, to explore the intellectual sources of Milton's ideas and images of happiness, or to seek, on the other hand, a master-symbolism (of light and darkness in Brooks; of Platonic personification of Mirth or Melancholy in Tuve)[5] governing the numerous disparate items included within the poem. A third strand of defensive criticism, responding to adverse remarks of T. S. Eliot about *L'Allegro*'s lack of particular observational detail,[6] has defended the stereotypical figures of the poem as proper to its universality. I should like to depart from these lines of criticism, and to look at this poem as an aesthetic object, rather than primarily as an ethical or intellectual one. (An aesthetic object employs ideas, but it uses them as raw material, just as it uses images or rhythms. All of the raw materials, including ideas, are made fundamentally subordinate to the law of aesthetic form being obeyed by the whole.) A poem of 150 lines can hardly be considered in real detail in a few pages, but I hope to mention the main psychological dimensions and aesthetic *trouvailles* of *L'Allegro*, since this poem best succeeds in carrying off, in a "perfect" way, the stylistic decorum and ethical insights of the young Milton.

L'Allegro

Hence loathèd Melancholy
    Of *Cerberus,* and blackest midnight born,
In *Stygian* Cave forlorn
    'Mongst horrid shapes, and shreiks, and sights unholy,
Find out som uncouth cell,
    Wher brooding darkness spreads his jealous wings,
And the night-Raven sings;
    There under *Ebon* shades, and low-brow'd Rocks,
As ragged as thy Locks,
    In dark *Cimmerian* desert ever dwell.

But com thou Goddes fair and free,
In Heav'n ycleap'd *Euphrosyne,*
And by men, heart-easing Mirth,
Whom lovely *Venus* at a birth
With two sister Graces more
To Ivy-crownèd *Bacchus* bore;
Or whether (as som Sager sing)
The frolick Wind that breathes the Spring,
Zephir with *Aurora* playing,

As he met her once a Maying,
There on Beds of Violets blew,
And fresh-blown Roses washt in dew,
Fill'd her with thee a daughter fair,
So bucksom, blith, and debonair.
Haste thee nymph, and bring with thee
Jest and youthful Jollity,
Quips and Cranks, and wanton Wiles,
Nods, and Becks, and Wreathèd Smiles,
Such as hang on *Hebe*'s cheek,
And love to live in dimple sleek;
Sport that wrincled Care derides,
And Laughter holding both his sides.
Com, and trip it as you go
On the light fantastick toe,
And in thy right hand lead with thee,
The Mountain Nymph, sweet Liberty;
And if I give thee honour due,
Mirth, admit me of thy crue
To live with her, and live with thee,
In unreprovèd pleasures free;
To hear the Lark begin his flight,
And singing startle the dull night,
From his watch-towre in the skies,
Till the dappled dawn doth rise;
Then to com in spight of sorrow,
And at my window bid good morrow,
Through the Sweet-Briar, or the Vine,
Or the twisted Eglantine.
While the Cock with lively din,
Scatters the rear of darknes thin,
And to the stack, or the Barn dore,
Stoutly struts his Dames before,
Oft list'ning how the Hounds and horn,
Chearly rouse the slumbring morn,

From the side of som Hoar Hill,
Through the high wood echoing shrill.
Som time walking not unseen
By Hedge-row Elms, on Hillocks green,
Right against the Eastern gate,
Wher the great Sun begins his state,
Rob'd in flames, and Amber light,
The clouds in thousand Liveries dight,
While the Plowman neer at hand,
Whistles ore the Furrow'd Land,
And the Milkmaid singeth blithe,
And the Mower whets his sithe,
And every Shepherd tells his tale
Under the Hawthorn in the dale.
Streit mine eye hath caught new pleasures
Whilst the Lantskip round it measures,
Russet Lawns, and Fallows Gray,
Where the nibling flocks do stray,
Mountains on whose barren brest
The labouring clouds do often rest:
Meadows trim with Daisies pide,
Shallow Brooks, and Rivers wide.
Towers, and Battlements it sees
Boosom'd high in tufted Trees,
Wher perhaps some beauty lies,
The Cynosure of neighbouring eyes.
Hard by, a Cottage chimney smokes,
From betwixt two aged Okes,
Where *Corydon* and *Thyrsis* met,
Are at their savory dinner set
Of Hearbs, and other Country Messes,
Which the neat-handed *Phillis* dresses;
And then in haste her Bowre she leaves,
With *Thestylis* to bind the Sheaves;
Or if the earlier season lead

To the tann'd Haycock in the Mead,
Som times with secure delight
The up-land Hamlets will invite,
When the merry Bells ring round,
And the jocond rebecks sound
To many a youth, and many a maid,
Dancing in the Chequer'd shade;
And young and old com forth to play
On a Sunshine Holyday,
Till the live-long day-light fail,
Then to the Spicy Nut-brown Ale,
With stories told of many a feat,
How *Faery Mab* the junkets eat,
She was pincht, and pull'd she sed,
And he by Friars Lanthorn led
Tells how the drudging *Goblin* swet,
To ern his Cream-bowle duly set,
When in one night, ere glimps of morn,
His shadowy Flale hath thresh'd the Corn
That ten day-labourers could not end,
Then lies him down the Lubbar Fend.
And stretch'd out all the Chimney's length,
Basks at the fire his hairy strength;
And Crop-full out of dores he flings,
Ere the first Cock his Mattin rings.
Thus don the Tales, to bed they creep,
By whispering Winds soon lull'd asleep.
Towred Cities please us then,
And the busie humm of men,
Where throngs of Knights and Barons bold,
In weeds of Peace high triumphs hold,
With store of Ladies, whose bright eies
Rain influence, and judge the prise
Of wit, or Arms, while both contend
To win her Grace, whom all commend.

There let *Hymen* oft appear
In Saffron robe, with Taper clear,
And pomp, and feast, and revelry,
With mask, and antique Pageantry,
Such sights as youthfull Poets dream
On Summer eeves by haunted stream.
Then to the well-trod stage anon,
If *Jonsons* learned Sock be on,
Or sweetest *Shakespear* fancies childe,
Warble his native Wood-notes wilde,
And ever against eating Cares,
Lap me in soft *Lydian* Aires,
Married to immortal verse
Such as the meeting soul may pierce
In notes, with many a winding bout
Of linckèd sweetnes long drawn out,
With wanton heed, and giddy cunning,
The melting voice through mazes running;
Untwisting all the chains that ty
The hidden soul of harmony.
That *Orpheus* self may heave his head
From golden slumber on a bed
Of heapt *Elysian* flowres, and hear
Such streins as would have won the ear
Of *Pluto,* to have quite set free
His half regain'd *Eurydice.*
These delights, if thou canst give,
Mirth with thee, I mean to live.

Let me first propose that there are four distinct parts to *L'Allegro* (although this poem has always been described, after its prologue, as merely a long list of things viewed by the protagonist). If one includes within the first part the opening 10-line rejection of black depression or "loathèd Melancholy" (Mirth's opposite), the 152-line poem seems to organize itself into roughly equal quarters of 40, 40, 36, and 36 lines:

L'Allegro: Chart of Proportions

Topic	Lines	Length	Gross Structure
Anathema:	1–10	10 lines	10 + 26 + 4 = 40
Invocation:	11–36	26 lines	
Refrain:	37–40	4 lines	
Sights & Sounds: (Day of Protagonist)	41–80	40 lines	40
Rustics: (Day and Evening)	81–116	36 lines	36
Cities and Music (Night of Protagonist)	117–150	34 lines	34 + 2 = 36
Refrain:	151–152	2 lines	
			Total: 152 lines

The first quarter—an introduction or prologue—is followed by the true "body" of the poem, which falls into three parts: the first recounts the *daytime* walk of the protagonist; the second, the *day and evening* activities of the rustics; and the third, the *evening* pleasures of the protagonist, closing with his praise of vocal music.

The happy man of the title—who speaks the whole poem—invokes (in the 30 lines following the 10-line introductory anathema) the goddess Euphrosyne or Mirth, offering alternate genealogies for her birth, and enumerating her attendants (of whom the chief is "sweet Liberty"); he ends the invocation by praying to be admitted among her crew, "To live with her, and live with thee, / In unreprovèd pleasures free." He will return to this refrain at the conclusion of the poem: "These delights, if thou canst give, / Mirth with thee, I mean to live." In between the two appearances of this refrain lie the last three quarters of the poem—its "body"—110 lines devoted to instancing "these delights." The aesthetic wager of the poem is that it can give us 110 lines of innocent delights without boring us. That is, it implicitly promises us successive tastes of the stylistically unexpected, the technically varied, and the thematically surprising.

Before coming to the 110-line body of the poem, we must consider how Milton, in the first 40 lines, establishes the large cosmological world in which he chooses to set his praise of Mirth. The most encompassing world of the poem is that of Greek myth, in which we meet not only the goddess Euphrosyne, but also Cerberus, the Homeric Cimmerian desert, Mirth's "sister Graces," and Bacchus, Venus, and Hebe. But Greek myth alone is not sufficient for Milton's inclusive cosmology: the second of the poem's enclosing spheres is the world of allegorical personifications, who exist in continuity with the Greek divinities. The "mountain nymph, sweet Liberty" is, as a nymph, close in character to the Grace she attends, while Zephyr and Aurora—natural presences, the breeze and the dawn—serve as transitional figures between myth and reality: though mythologically named, they are elements of the actual physical world. The personified Liberty, because she is called a nymph, belongs also to mythology: she affords a conceptual bridge from mythology to Milton's simpler, non-mythological personifications of human sociability and behavior, such as Jest, Sport, "wrincled Care," and "Laughter holding both his sides." We can conclude from Milton's addition of these "English" figures that the conceptual world of Greek myth does not wholly suffice as ethical context for the sort of Mirth that he wishes to illustrate.

Since the Greek mythological genealogy of Euphrosyne that Milton cites (derived from Renaissance dictionaries)[7] asserts that Mirth is born from the conjunction of Venereal pleasure and Bacchic intoxication, Greece does not in this respect suit the young Milton's chaste idealism. In offering an alternate, and preferred, genealogy—asserting that Mirth issues from the union of the west wind and the dawn, as a fleeting caress inspires auroral conception—Milton offers a critique of Greece, but prefers to improve its genealogy rather than discard it as an imaginative surround. Since Milton in this poem is examining natural man engaged in innocent pleasures of both body and spirit, the pagan sexual context of the conjoining of Zephyr and Aurora suits the theme (to which a Christian context, with its ultimately ascetic dimension, would be alien). In fact, when Milton takes up contemplative pleasure in *Il Penseroso,* the Christian context immediately troubles the values earlier examined in *L'Allegro,* so much so that one can't simply view these poems as presenting the same person alternately and equably participating in mirth one day and contemplation the next. The critical view that treats one poem as a "stepping-stone" to the other implicitly asserts that one can't go backward from the contemplative position to the mirthful one. This attitude places the "Greek" pleasures of *L'Allegro* in a position of subordination, whereas those pleasures, I think, deserve (since they occur in a free-standing work which achieves its own closure) to be considered separately rather than comparatively.

After the initial appearance of Greek mythology in the anathema and invocation, Greece returns four more times in *L'Allegro,* and these appearances suggest why Milton retained Greek thought here as the most comprehensive outer circle of his poetic universe. Greece arrives for the second time in the person of the rustics, who are given the Greek (though Virgil-derived) names of Corydon, Phyllis, and Thestylis: in short, Milton offers Greece as the guaranteeing origin of pastoral, since *L'Allegro* is largely a pastoral poem. In its third appearance, Greece gives the poem its theoretical musical mode: "And ever against eating cares, / Lap me in soft Lydian airs." Those airs, as the *Variorum* informs us, were contrasted in Greek musical theory to "the martial Phyrgian and solemn Dorian," and were sometimes (but not here) considered sentimental.[8] Greece presides as well, in its critical fourth appearance, over the protagonist's sexual potential, which, though not acted out, is anticipated by the appearance of saffron-robed Hymen, god of marriage. And for its last manifestation, Greece returns in the climactic figure of Orpheus, who, by illustrating the power of song even in the gloomy domain of Pluto, guarantees the worth of the poetic vocation. The Renaissance protagonist, with characteristic Miltonic competitiveness, will outdo Orpheus, since "the melting voice through mazes running" will produce such "streins as would have won the ear / Of *Pluto,* to have quite set free / His half-regain'd *Eurydice*."[9] (In *Il Penseroso,* Milton will set secular poetry—represented by Orpheus and Chaucer—lower than spiritual music, the cloister, the organ, the hermitage, and prophecy.)

In the middle of *L'Allegro,* enclosed by the divine world of Greek myth and the conceptual world of allegorical personification which between them supervise the poem, we find the double natural world of country and city, as Milton tells us that the happy man needs both rural and urban pleasures to make up his count. *L'Allegro* gains its expansiveness from its long inventory of pleasures, and we can learn a great deal about Milton's aesthetic aims from examining this middle part of the poem. The happy man, significantly, doesn't keep the civilized and the natural in separate compartments: he in fact normally has recourse to the cultural as a metaphor for the natural. The lark sings from "his watch-towre in the skies"; the cock "scatters the rear" of the defeated army of darkness and struts before his "Dames"; the "great Sun" in his robes is attended, in his "state," by the clouds clad "in thousand Liveries." In the mind of the speaker, the natural is interpenetrated by the cultural, just as the landscape of the morning scene is interrupted by the civilized horn of the hunt. Nature, here, is not pre-human but integrated with civilized thought and reference, just as it is, in a different respect, integrated with mythological fancy and personified spirits. The fullest mark of the integration of the natural with the cultural comes when the eye of the happy man strays from landscape to the architecture that the landscape encloses, speculating whether those "Towers, and Battlements" conceal a beauty within. One of the most winning aspects of the young Milton's mind is this effortless accommodation of the civilized within the natural, and the enclosure of both within the overseeing presence of the imaginative. In Milton's ideal world, where Zephyr plays with Aurora to generate Mirth, the happy man's glance can encompass, in a single day, the sun, beauty's tower, allegorical Liberty, peasants dancing in the chequered shade, and Shakespeare's woodnotes wild, all serenely coexisting.

It's not difficult to imagine a manner of description that would refrain from obvious human reference, refusing *L'Allegro*'s implicit assertion of an easy compatibility between the civilized and the natural. If we were to delete the human metaphors of the morning passage—taking "startle" and "watch-towre" away from the lark; "dull" from the night; "scatters the rear" and "stoutly struts" and "Dames" from the cock; "gate," "state," "rob'd," and "Liveries" from the sun; and "Amber" from the clouds—we would arrive at a more purely visual—and much duller—description:

Metaphorical	Dis-Figured
To hear the Lark begin his flight,	To hear the Lark begin his flight,
And singing startle the dull night,	And singing sound through the dark night
From his watch-towre in the skies . . .	From his place in lofty skies . . .
While the Cock with lively din	While the Cock with lively din
Scatters the rear of darknes thin,	Crows in the midst of darknes thin,
And to the stack, or the Barn dore,	And at the stack, or the Barn dore,
Stoutly struts his Dames before . . .	Joins his hens and goes before . . .
Right against the Eastern gate,	Right against the Eastern way,
Wher the great Sun begins his state,	Where the bright Sun begins his day,
Rob'd in flames and Amber light,	Set in flames and yellow light,
The clouds in thousand Liveries dight.	The clouds assembling at his height.

Not only could we remove the civilized and anthropomorphizing human reference from natural description, we could imagine the rural portion of *L'Allegro* stripped of towers and battlements, remaining a pure natural landscape as far as the eye could see. But Milton keeps his pastoral scene metaphorically humanized and architecturally inhabited, arguing implicitly for the seamless juncture, in the modern mind, of birds and sentries, cocks and patriarchs, suns and monarchs, lawns and battlements.

Because of the entire imaginative compatibility between the rural and the civilized implied by the young poet's lines, we rightly expect that after glimpsing towers and battlements (in line 77), the happy man will proceed away from nature in order to explore the offerings of culture. Eventually—in line 117, where the protagonist's evening begins—this will happen, though in the first person plural: "Towred Cities please *us* then [emphasis mine]." But much intervenes between the two mentions of towers. What has kept the protagonist from proceeding directly from his daytime rural towers in line 77 to his evening towered cities in line 117? And what purpose is served by this long interruption of his progress through a single day?

Strangely enough, the intervening lines—which make up the third quarter of the poem (ll. 80–116)—introduce into its narrative the day and evening of an entirely new set of human *dramatis personae,* an episode unforeseeable by anyone reading the poem up to this point. Because the poem is called *L'Allegro,* its protagonist must be a single person (as Dr. Johnson first pointed out in adverting to the solitude of the speaker); and we will see the single protagonist return, not only as he is included in the first-person plural of "Towred Cities please us then" and the third-person surrogate mention of "youthfull Poets," but eventually as his first-person self, when he says "Lap me in soft *Lydian* Aires" and "Mirth with thee, I mean to live." But his own first-person self and actions are displaced—for a full quarter of the poem—by other selves, other actions. Who are the new actors who draw Milton's attention away from his solitary protagonist? They are the Greek-named rustics, and they and their companions experience a day and an evening paralleling the protagonist's own. Both his actions and theirs are habitual ("sometimes" doing this, "oft" doing that). The peasants of Part III act out four sets of typical life-motions: they consume a meal; they work in the fields making hay or (in a later season) binding sheaves; they dance in couples to the music of rebecks; and they tell stories.

We recognize, after some thought, that the rustics are in the poem to carry out actions unsuitable for ascription to the cultivated protagonist. Yet the first three actions ascribed to the rustics are surely indispensable to anyone's ordinary happiness: men and women leading the usual active life eat and work and couple and divert themselves in dance. However, these actions are the province of what philosophy used to call the "baser" senses of taste and smell and touch:

and once we see that the activities of these senses are reserved to the rustics, we recognize that Milton's protagonist exercises only the "higher" or "theoretical" senses of sight and hearing. Within the poem, he does not engage in work; nor does he eat or drink (though a "feast" is anticipated in dream); nor is he placed as yet in a sexual relation (though his marriage is anticipated in the jussive, "There let *Hymen* oft appear"). The division of leisure and labor, of higher and lower senses, is absolute here, and the poet finds that he must register a functional separation between his educated wanderer and the rustic peasants.

Yet Milton gives his peasants as much human dignity as he allows to his protagonist: their dinner diffuses a savory odor; Phillis is "neat-handed"; their bells are merry, their rebecks jocund (they create instrumental music); their holiday is a sunshine one; and their play is engaged in with "secure delight" as they are seen dancing (they have aesthetic practices) "in the Chequer'd shade." The poet, that is, will sequester in the persons of the rustics the sensuous activities of smell, taste, and touch without denigrating these actions—or the act of work—as sources of happiness. Those who object to what they see as pastoral's "mystification" of the world of hard agricultural work mistake Milton's aim in the poem, which is not a realistic depiction of farm labor, but a symbolic design for presenting the pleasures of the senses. Though their names tell us that the ploughman ploughs and the milkmaid milks, these figures are represented here as whistling and singing, contributing the human aesthetic supplement to "servile labor," thereby rendering their actions, however effortful, different from that of the ox who pulls the plough or that of the calf that suckles at its mother. Milton intends, in presenting his rustics, a hymn to the activities of the body when they are carried out in a happy state. It is true that he allots those sensuous activities, in this poem, to rustics whose vocation does not resemble his own intellectual one. Yet he insists, by portraying the rustics' day and evening, on including sensuous pleasures, lovingly described, among the "unreprovèd pleasures free."

At this point the poet stops for reflection. He has already implied, in the rustics' love of song and music, a resemblance to himself: is there no connection between himself as writer and the countrymen? In a remarkable expansion of the rustics' evening, Milton now gives his rustics literary ability, displaying their skill in narrative and the perpetuation of verbal composition in an oral community. At the end of their day of work, the peasants give free rein to their imagination in competitive antiphonal tales: "She was pincht, and pull'd she sed, / And he by Friars Lanthorn led / Tells how the drudging *Goblin* swet, / To ern his Cream-bowle duly set."[10] Ethically, this telling of tales supplies a human connection between the cultivated protagonist and the illiterate rustics, establishing an aesthetic continuity of imagination and narration between the two social orders. What is most winning in the young Milton's passage on oral literature (besides his linking the rural imagination to Shakespeare by reference to the rustics' mention of "fairy Mab") is his own implied entrancement with folk narration, as he spiritedly reproduces, in free indirect discourse, the tale of the goblin as excitedly told in hyperboles under the influence of the nut-brown ale. The peasant narrator

> Tells how the drudging *Goblin* swet,
> To ern his Cream-bowle duly set,
> When in one night, ere glimps of morn,
> His shadowy Flale hath thresh'd the Corn
> That ten day-labourers could not end;
> Then lies him down the Lubbar Fend.
> And stretch'd out all the Chimney's length,
> Basks at the fire his hairy strength;
> And Crop-full out of dores he flings,
> Ere the first Cock his Mattin rings.

This account of the goblin is, amazingly, the longest single excursus in the body of the poem. The goblin is given more lines than Orpheus, more space than the drama of Jonson and Shakespeare. This proportioning of Milton's attention is surely remarkable, and worth comment.

Let us return for a moment to the questions with which we began:

How does a young poet come of age? How does he find the stylistic maturity that must, in his case, parallel and enable his access to psychological maturity? We have seen that Milton has already begun to think through the relation of classical and Christian material. In *L'Allegro,* he has found a way of sequestering, without criticism, the pagan or natural life from the life ordered according to Christian practice. (Earlier, in the Nativity Ode, he had used the return of the classical Golden Age as a parallel to Christian eschatology, and at the same time opposed Christian to pagan deities; later, in *Lycidas,* he will—temporarily—find a way to unite symbiotically the classical and the Christian.) Of course Milton had poetic precedent, especially in Spenser, for these three strategies: *L'Allegro*'s segregation of one order of belief from another; the Nativity Ode's paralleling and opposition of orders; and *Lycidas*' syncretism. But even if he has inherited marvelous models, a young writer must think about and think through those models in order to use them intelligently. It was from Shakespeare and Jonson that Milton had learned to combine English fairy lore with classical allusions, yet the passage on the goblin in *L'Allegro* feels no need to announce its literary origins: it fits seamlessly into the continuing portrait of the rustic day and evening. Milton's sheer pleasure in the exaggerations and suspense of folk narration and in the grotesquerie of the hairy goblin gives us a glimpse of his love of all literary manifestations, rustic as well as educated. He feels no superciliousness vis-à-vis the peasants: their evening relish in telling tales is matched by the subsequent evening delight of the literate protagonist in his visits to the theater. As Milton allows the tale of the goblin to dilate, we feel that the poem has momentarily "escaped" authorial discipline, that the moment of rustic tale-telling is prolonging itself in an aesthetic indulgence granted by the sympathetic author of the poem. If *L'Allegro* did not exemplify (as well as assert) the presence of pleasure of both "high" and "low" literary efforts, it could hardly convince us of the truth of its thematic justifying of both the "higher" and the "lower" senses.

The superstitious tales of the rustics are told not only through awed hyperboles, but also through energetic verbals: *eat, pinched, pulled, led, sweat, earn, thresh, end, stretch, flings, rings.* This marshaling of grammatical activity shows us the young poet in full control of his extended effect. These strenuous verbals are different from the sedate verbs so far associated with the protagonist: *to live, to hear, to come, [to] bid, listening, walking.* A true writer feels his verbals kinesthetically: imaginatively, he winces with "pinch," hurls with "flings," strains with "earn," and measures to each situation its quantum of energy. Already we see Milton in full command of such energy-allotting. And a true writer takes the "temperature" or "feel" of words. With exact pleasure we hear "lap" in "Lap me in soft *Lydian* Aires" or the Shakespearean "nibbling" in "the nibling flocks": each is perfectly calibrated in tender "feel" to its moment. Milton is no less generous in minuscule pleasing effects both graphic and phonetic, as any passage chosen at random will show. Even neglecting the more subtle metrical effects connecting one line to another,[11] we find in any characteristic excerpt, if we read it aloud, few phonemes or letters that are not audibly or visually bound to some other.

If the giving or withholding of kinetic energy in words, the conferring of the right "temperature" or "feel" on a phrase, and the able but unintrusive insertion of recursive phonetic and graphic forms are three aspects of a young poet's mastery, the managing of rhythm is equally important. Milton's advance in perfecting the Jonsonian tetrameter can be seen in the confidence of the rhythms of *L'Allegro* compared to those of his earlier tetrameter poem, *Epitaph on the Marchioness of Winchester.* Often, in the *Epitaph,* there are infelicities of rhythm, as with the conferring of theoretical stress on the first syllable of "besides" in line 4 (emphasis mine):

> This rich marble doth inter
> The honoured wife of Winchester,
> A viscount's daughter, an earl's heir,
> *Be*sides what her virtues fair
> Added to her noble birth.

In the *Epitaph,* too, sometimes insufficient intonational direction is given, so that one can at first make a mistake in the accentuation of a line. "Her high birth, and her graces sweet" can be commenced "*Her* high *birth,* and" (as if the first foot were a trochee) until we are made to understand, halfway through the line, that the initial foot is an iamb, and we must read "Her *high* birth, *and* her *graces* sweet." Similarly, one can begin by reading "*Plucked* up *by* some" as trochees in "So have I seen some tender slip . . . / Plucked up by some unheedy swain," not discovering till we reach "unheedy" that "Plucked *up*" and "by *some*" are iambs. Had the line read "Plucked up by some needy swain," our first intonation would have proved correct. There are no such radical ambiguities of intonation present in *L'Allegro.*[12] On the contrary: nothing about *L'Allegro* is more convincing (after the deliberately irregular opening anathema) than its untroubled and lilting cascade of beautiful tetrameters:

> Streit mine eye hath caught new pleasures
> Whilst the Lantskip round it measures,
> Russet Lawns, and Fallows Gray,
> Where the nibling flocks do stray,
> Mountains on whose barren brest
> The labouring clouds do often rest:
> Meadows trim with Daisies pide,
> Shallow Brooks, and Rivers wide.

Such a passage chooses to emphasize the trochaic potential of tetrameter, while another might chiefly emphasize its iambic possibilities:

> And then in haste her Bowre she leaves,
> With *Thestylis* to bind the Sheaves,
> Or if the earlier season lead
> To the tann'd Haycock in the Mead,
> Som times with secure delight
> The up-land Hamlets will invite, . . .
> And young and old come forth to play
> On a Sunshine Holyday.

These changes are not dictated by content so much as by the poet's wish to leave off one sustained metrical emphasis and begin another for the sake of musicality. In trochaic passages Milton will often insert an iambic line ("The labouring clouds do often rest") or in iambic passages a trochaic initial foot ("Som times with secure delight") to keep the internal variation-principle afloat.

But it is time to come back to the body of our poem. The poet, having observed the rustics through their characteristic day and evening activities in Part III, has lulled them to sleep, and so can return in Part IV to his cultivated protagonist, who, having left behind his daytime pleasures (where we last saw him contemplating towers among trees) is now encountering, as his evening begins, "the busy hum of men" in "towered cities." Triumphs and the contests of wit and arms (with verdicts given by the attendant ladies) are succeeded by the somewhat perplexing appearance of Hymen. I take this figure, as I have said, to represent the as yet unactualized sexual potential of the protagonist, which will be realized in marriage. The euphemized rustic "dance" of "many a man and many a maid" has not yet found its equivalent in the life of the happy man, but by mentioning the person of Hymen, Milton inserts the fulfillment of sexual desire in marriage into the list of Mirth's licit "delights." Just as Hymen is a figure of sexual potential, so the youthful poets who "dream" of "pomp, and feast, and revelry, / With mask, and antique Pageantry" are figures of imaginative potential, conjured up in reverie by young artists before their own art finds embodied form. Although the protagonist's attendance at comedies by Jonson or Shakespeare hints that eventually he may himself become a composer of literature, Milton sets, as the highest of all the arts, not literature but vocal music. The rustics had only their homemade rebecks, their folk songs, and their oral tales; but the speaker of *L'Allegro* desires complex vocal music, "*Lydian* Aires, / Married to immortal verse."

The choices of the protagonist in Part IV all represent forms of sophisticated art. They include—in order of rising dignity—ritual art (in contests of wit or arms), liturgical art (in Hymen saffron-robed and carrying his taper), courtly art (in masque and pageantry), dramatic art (in Jonson and Shakespeare), and masterpieces of musico-poetic art (the verse to which the Lydian melodies are married is said to be "immortal"). Such a determined hierarchical order—even if expressed with the "oft's" and "or's" of speculative verse—shows us a young poet firmly in command of his own values and their rank-order, up to the highest. It is in the description of vocal music that Milton's lexicon becomes most reverberant and gifted. The intrinsic qualities of high art are evoked, one by one, as Milton emphasizes, with respect to music, its emotionality by the verb "pierce"; its sweetness by the participial adjective "melting"; its complexity in the image of "mazes"; its power in the strength of the participial phrase "untwisting all the chains"; and its headiness by the unexpected oxymorons in the "wanton" nature of its "heed" and the "giddy" nature of its "cunning." To have resolved that art must combine emotion, sweetness, complexity, power, care, cunning, and spontaneity is to have thought long and hard about the qualities present in admirable aesthetic composition.

This is perhaps the moment in which to recall, by a glance at this passage on music, the young Milton's easy management of enjambments and caesuras in *L'Allegro*. The airs he desires are those

> Such as the meeting soul may pierce
> In notes, with many a winding bout
> Of linckèd sweetnes long drawn out,
> With wanton heed, and giddy cunning,
> The melting voice through mazes running,
> Untwisting all the chains that ty
> The hidden soul of harmony.

The enjambments as the soul is pierced and as the bouts deliver their linkèd sweetness are countered by the internal pauses after "notes" and "heed"; and the caesura in the second line arrives after two syllables, while the one in the fourth line occurs after four syllables, obeying Milton's usual principle of pleasing musical variation. Needless to say, the *m*'s and *n*'s of this exquisitely "melting" passage are intuitive if not deliberate.

What, then, has the young Milton learned and practiced in order to create an individual style and to write a "perfect" poem? He has become aware of the problem inherent in the coexistence of his two "master narratives," that of Greek myth and that of Christianity, and has thought about ways to evade, present, or solve that problem (here, by suppressing Christianity altogether). He can summon (and revise) ancient myths, create and cluster allegorical personifications, and mix social types, as it suits his purpose. He is conscious of the alternate worlds of oral and written literature: the imagination of the folk voiced in expressive tales and the literate imagination embodied in masques and dramas. He has made an inventory of the chief forms of innocent human happiness in the active (by contrast to the contemplative) life, and has worried about how to include them all. To solve that difficulty, he has decided to restrict the protagonist of *L'Allegro* to activities of the "higher" senses of sight and hearing, and to sequester, within tableaux of rustics, the acting out of the forms of happiness proper to the "lower senses"—while not deleting, from the world of his protagonist, anticipation of feasts and eventual sexual pleasure, and not deleting, from the world of the rustics, the "higher" pleasures of sight and hearing. Yet, wary of too absolute an ethical division between "lower" and "higher" senses, Milton has allowed his rustics to take pleasure—in addition to their enjoyment of all the senses—in their participation in the making of art. They have their singing (in the person of the milkmaid), their instrumental music (in their rebecks), and their imagination (in their tales), all of which bring about a human rapprochement between the plane on which the rustics live and the plane on which Milton imagines his protagonist to exist, thus allowing the poet to maintain an ethical attitude of human respect and human connection toward all his *dramatis personae*. And Milton has carried out this scheme by means of a classically-proportioned four-part poem, with the parts almost equal in length, in which the separated day and evening activities of the protagonist act as brackets, fore and aft, to the conjoined day and evening activities of the rustics. A chiastic *abba* structural arrangement (by contrast to the more "natural" linear one) is always, in poetry, the sign of forethought and pre-arrangement. Here it marks the young

Milton's devising of a plan by which the repetition of pleasures—which could have fallen into predictability—instead retains surprise.

Above all, Milton has found in this poem what will be his master tropes: extension in time and space, and enumeration of the ingredients of some conceived plenitude. The poem—after its initial anathema of Melancholy—is an inventory of inventories, a list of lists, extending over the day and night, rustic and urban, of the protagonist, and over the day and night, in the fields and in the cottage, of the rustics. As the great poet of plenitude, Milton will later populate heaven, earth, and hell, from Creation to the Last Trump, with people and places and activities and discourses. But here he makes formal lists, in sequence, of many things: the alternative sets of parents of Mirth; the companions of Euphrosyne; the beauties of nature; the activities of rustics; the tales told by the folk; the cultural allurements of cities; the works of modern dramatists; and the ecstasies of vocal music set to immortal texts. The last is hardly a list: it goes beyond enumeration in its entwinements of effect.

L'Allegro gives evidence that the young Milton has mastered the resources of syntax. He has kept syntax simple in many of his lists, as he does in the short phrases enumerating Mirth's attendants:

> Haste thee nymph, and bring with thee
> Jest and youthful Jollity,
> Quips and Cranks, and wanton Wiles,
> Nods, and Becks, and Wreathèd Smiles.

Nothing could be more artless than this paratactic linking by "and."

The next step up in lengthening a list is to apportion its members to distinct couplets. These tend to exhibit parallel syntax; here, the coupled nouns—lawns and fallows, mountains and meadows—are all followed by modifying clauses or phrases naming their "populations"—flocks, clouds, and daisies:

> Russet Lawns, and Fallows Gray,
> Where the nibling flocks do stray,

> Mountains on whose barren breast
> The labouring clouds do often rest:
> Meadows trim with Daisies pide,
> Shallow Brooks, and Rivers wide.[13]

Both of these syntactically simple passages are a far cry from the superbly unfolding hypotactic syntax that closes the poem:

> And ever against eating Cares,
> Lap me in soft *Lydian* Aires,
> Married to immortal verse
> Such as the meeting soul may pierce
> In notes, with many a winding bout
> Of linckèd sweetnes long drawn out,
> With wanton heed, and giddy cunning,
> The melting voice through mazes running,
> Untwisting all the chains that ty
> The hidden soul of harmony.

If we graph this sentence, we can see its enchained nature:

Lap me in Aires
    married to verse
        such as the soul may pierce
            in notes
                with many a bout of sweetnes
                    long drawn out,

With wanton heed,
   and
  giddy cunning, The melting voice
           through mazes running,
               Untwisting all the chains
                  that ty the soul.

This complex imitative syntax, twisting and untwisting its grammatical chains, disabuses us of any idea that *L'Allegro* is an artless and naïve poem, as it might have seemed if we judged it (as many seem to do when they think it inferior to *Il Penseroso*) only by its earlier and simpler lists of Mirth's companions, or by those one-line stereotypical pastoral figures criticized by Eliot. By matching his syntax to its correspondent pleasures, Milton assures us that the multiple forms of happiness can range from the shortest and most immediate to the most complicated and through-composed.

The young Milton has also learned an evenness of tone. Nothing in the voicing of the initial serene pastoral walk betrays the fact that we'll later encounter either goblins or madrigalesque ecstasies, not to speak of Shakespeare's comedies. The journey we are afforded by the poem keeps, each sequestered in its moment, its various levels of pleasure. It is for this reason that we are so often surprised: What, Corydon and Thyrsis are here? And a lubber fiend too? Then back to Greece with Hymen! But Jonson is in the wings! And can this be Eurydice? The charm of the poem lies in such unexpected appearances, which, through the remarkable evenness of tone of the whole as it progresses, succeed each other with no instability, eccentricity, or alarm. Milton has learned to slip from one compartment of his mind to another without strain, and with temperate pleasure—until he capitulates to a final intensity, the ecstatic feeling that arises when verse and music are combined.

Milton by now has investigated and arranged his myths and personified values; the rustic and civilized planes of social existence, diurnal and nocturnal; the active (versus the contemplative) life; his artistic hierarchy of value; his architectonic structures; and his ethical obligations. He is ready to claim his right to unreprovèd pleasures, and to assert his personal enumeration of such pleasures, from those of sexuality to those of the eye and ear. Technically speaking, he has mastered rhythm and phrasing and syntax; he has found a low, a middle, and a high style, and a way to include—by judicious separation within the poem—both the humor of his strutting cock and the passion of Orpheus and Eurydice. He has given enumerative distinctiveness to each of his lists, and has practiced forms of variation in his dancing tetrameters.[14] He knows the resources of syntax, and can invent firm grammatical structures, both simple and complex, on which to construct the body of his poem. He has achieved both surprise of subject and steadiness of tone. In one sense, he has nothing more to learn; and the masterpiece that is *L'Allegro* tells us that he has, both psychologically and technically, arrived at a seductive and complex representation of life extended widely in time, space, and social strata. A sterner and more opulent form of mastery, already somewhat awkwardly nascent in the Nativity Ode, awaits its perfection in *Paradise Lost.*

2

JOHN KEATS

Perfecting the Sonnet

The flower must drink the nature of the soil
    Before it can put forth its blossoming.
       (*Spenser, a jealous honorer of thine,* 5 February 1818)[1]

If by dull rhymes our English must be chain'd,
    And, like Andromeda, the sonnet sweet
       Fetter'd, in spite of painèd loveliness;
Let us find out, if we must be constrain'd,
    Sandals more interwoven and complete
To fit the naked foot of Poesy:
       Let us inspect the lyre, and weigh the stress
Of every chord, and see what may be gain'd
    By ear industrious, and attention meet;
       Misers of sound and syllable, no less
Than Midas of his coinage, let us be
    Jealous of dead leaves in the bay wreath crown;
So, if we may not let the muse be free,
    She will be bound with garlands of her own.
       (*On the Sonnet,* end April/early May 1819)

K EATS enters the anthologies with a sonnet—*On First Looking into Chapman's Homer*—which has become the most famous of his early poems, and which will be the central subject of this essay. Keats is an example of the young poet who finds his voice by persistently composing in a single inherited form—in Keats's case, the sonnet—until he has made it his own. He is already thinking of this form as one of his chief fields of endeavor when, at twenty-one, he begins to assemble work for his first volume, the *Poems* published in March of 1817. In the table of contents of this volume, the verses are grouped by genre under three categories—"Poems," "Epistles," and "Sonnets"—among which sonnets are the dominant cluster: there are 21 of them in the book.[2]

By contrast, Keats's second volume, *Lamia and Other Poems,* issued in 1820, confines itself to narrative poems, ballads, and odes. It contains, surprisingly, no sonnets at all, even though Keats had finished and kept some 32 sonnets between 1817 and 1820. He had allowed six of those 32 sonnets to be published either in journals or in Leigh Hunt's yearly anthology called the *Pocket-Book,* but he suppressed even the already published sonnets from his 1820 volume. He no longer wished to be identified with sonnets: they were too acutely reminiscent of Leigh Hunt, from whose poetry he had distanced himself. Writing to Benjamin Robert Haydon in March 1818, he remarked, "It is a great Pity that People should by associating themselves with the fine[st] things, spoil them—Hunt has damned Hampstead [and] Masks and Sonnets and italian tales" (L, I, 252). (Nonetheless, the volume of 1820 revealed what Keats had learned by writing sonnets, since the 10-line stanza he invents for several of the odes appends a Petrarchan sestet to a Shakespearean quatrain, hybridizing his two inherited sonnet forms.)[3]

When we look back to Keats's first sonnets, we see that they are confined to the Petrarchan form (if we except two very early experiments with hybrids). After much practice (summarized in my appendix on the pre-*1817* sonnets at the end of this chapter), he composes the strikingly mature Petrarchan sonnet *On First Looking into Chapman's Homer,* which has become a canonical poem of British Romanticism. Some of the other sonnets in *Poems 1817*—such as *Keen, fitful gusts* and *On the Grasshopper and Cricket*—remain among Keats's most frequently anthologized poems, and I'll turn to them as context for *Chapman's Homer.* In spite of these Petrarchan successes, Keats does not remain content with what he has accomplished; in 1818, at twenty-two, he begins with a passion to compose Shakespearean sonnets, both in the received form and in variants of it that he invents (see the appended chronological chart of post-*1817* composition).

We can say, then, that Keats finds himself as a young lyric poet through apprenticing himself to the Petrarchan sonnet. Though he never drops that form altogether, his principled adoption of Shakespearean tragic values after the 1818 publication of his long romance *Endymion* marks a distinct change in his moral (and consequently literary) affiliation. After 1818, Shakespeare moves into the ascendant—over Petrarch, Spenser, and Chatterton—and the Shakespearean sonnet becomes Keats's vehicle of choice (though even then, as my second epigraph shows, Keats continues to experiment in the sonnet form). Although the post-*1817* work falls, strictly speaking, outside my aim of showing Keats's first perfect work, I'll briefly consider the manifesto-in-sonnet-form that records his turn to Shakespeare, *On Sitting Down to Read King Lear Once Again,* because in that sonnet Keats judges, and criticizes, the earlier poems that are my subject here.

How does Keats come to his eventual superb ease of manner in the Petrarchan sonnet? To do so, he has to learn to use effectively the binary nature of the sonnet, to find accurate and emotionally authentic symbols of his feelings, to achieve a combination of intimacy and objectivity with respect to the outer world, to make words enact (rhythmically, syntactically, phonetically) their assertions, to minimize egotism, and to press the sonnet as far as it can go toward a personal style, on the one hand, and to an epic reach, on the other. Why did the form of the sonnet so attract Keats? What were Keats's errors and successes in the non-tragic mode of his early Petrarchan sonnet-practice? And how does he put himself to school so that he can—by twenty-one—write lasting poems in this form? Finally, why is he compelled to turn definitively, at twenty-two, to Shakespeare as his model?

Keats is drawn to the Petrarchan sonnet by the example of his early mentor, Leigh Hunt,[4] but unlike Hunt, he is imaginatively interested from the beginning in the inherent malleability of the form. His first extant sonnet *(On Peace)* grafts an irregular Petrarchan sestet onto a Shakespearean octave; it also violates the rules of the sonnet-form by continuing into the sestet a rhyme-sound found in the octave: *abab cdcd ddedee.* And although most of the lines of *On Peace* have five beats, Keats defies the normative pentameter by giving seven beats to line 9, and six beats to line 14. In short, Keats, unlike Hunt, launches himself into the form as into a workshop, never to cease experimenting.

The sonnet offers to Keats not only the variety of its forms, but also the attraction of both following (and revising) its perennial themes. While under Hunt's influence, Keats sometimes explores, in and out of sonnets, political subjects—Leigh Hunt's imprisonment, the 1660 Restoration, Kosciusko—but his most frequent early concerns remain those of the Renaissance sonnet: love, friendship, and art. We can see Keats thinking out his positions on these intense topics throughout his sonnet work, often in the dialectic of inner debate prompted and seconded by the binary Petrarchan form.

Although Keats loved poetic narrative, especially its two extremes—the spare ballad and the digressive tale—he was perhaps intrinsically more a meditative poet than a narrative one, and the sonnet is irresistible as a flexible container for meditation. Keats knew the effort made by Milton and Wordsworth to modernize the sonnet and expand its formal and thematic range, and his ambition led him to continue the effort of those daunting poets. By the end of his life, he had succeeded in adding notably to the renewal of the sonnet, questioning its inherited neo-Platonic axioms, rearranging its rhymes, and humanizing its diction. How did he learn—in the first part of his short career—to be original in his treatment of the sonnet's themes, to become at home in its intellectual demands, and to modify its architectonic and rhyming forms?

I will begin at the worst and rise toward the best, though Keats's own early trajectory is one of ups and downs. He has resolved to master the Petrarchan form, and before the publication of his first *Poems* he has written and kept (as the appended chart of pre-*1817* composition shows) 30 Petrarchan sonnets. As we read these chronologically, we see him struggling at first simply to obey the rules of the octave, to find four *a* rhymes and fou*r* *b* rhymes. Once he has found them, he is thrifty in recycling them: the *fair, air,* and *impair* of sonnet 2 (the numbers refer to the chronological list of Keats's sonnets in my appendix) turn up in exactly the same order in 5; the *fate* and *elate* of sonnet 4 turn up immediately in 5; the *rest* and *drest* of 7 reappear in 12; the *dell* and *swell* of 9 are put to use in 10. I could cite more, but the point is made.

Yet even as Keats relies on conventional rhymes, he begins to imagine better ones. The first few extant sonnets naturally make use of easily found and common monosyllables (such as *love* and *dove*), but as early as *Woman! when I behold thee* (sonnet 6) we can mark a striking advance, as Keats begins to search for interesting (that is, unpredictable) rhymes. The sestet rhymes in 6, for instance—none of them self-evident or foreseeable—are the unexpected *tender, adore, defender, Calidore, Leander,* and *yore.* But a more profound advance (because it is a moral one) is visible in 7 (*Light feet,* a poem about his susceptibility to women) in which Keats is looking for a rhyme for *lark* and *mark.* He could have found a way to use, as his final rhyme, something thematically suitable for this poem: *dark* or *hark.* Instead, the rhyme-word is—absurdly—*shark.* Keats chooses, crucially, to follow the path of his intended meaning even if it makes for incongruity. He has been speaking of his susceptibility to women's physical charm, which (he says in self-reproach) he cannot ignore, even when it is not "drest / In . . . virtues rare." But when he finds intelligence as well, in the person of a woman whose talk does not bore or disgust him, his ear (he adds, finding his rhyme for *lark*), "is open like a greedy shark / To catch the tunings of a voice divine." That greedy shark—preposterous as it is—testifies to Keats's wish to tell the candid truth about his appetitiveness for the sound of beautiful and intelligent language. A less truthful or more timid poet would have canceled the shark in favor of a more decorous rhyme, but Keats refuses to sacrifice exactness to decorum.

The early sonnets are often insignificant, derivative, and sentimental. Yet already, in the first 15 sonnets that have come down to us, Keats has tried out as many as seven sonnet-types (H_S, P_{2a}, P_1, P_{3a}, P_{2a+}, P_4, and H_P, to use the shorthand of my appended chart of his sonnet-types). His first known sonnet, as I've said, is a hybrid of Shakespearean and Petrarchan units; and within his prevalent Petrarchan mode, where the octave-form is inflexible, he assiduously varies, from sonnet to sonnet, the arrangement of syntax and rhyme in the sestet—a form of work invisible to the casual eye, but indispensable to the apprentice poet. He is also amassing experience in managing the articulation of octave to sestet: he may make the whole sonnet a single sentence, for example; or he may break it into asymmetrical or enjambed sentence-units that contest the rhyme-units of octave and sestet. These experiments are carried out in the service of feeling, as Keats searches for means to express a sequence of emotions, emotions that have been strong enough to compel him from silence into composition.

It matters to Keats not only what a sonnet says but the way it sounds as spoken utterance. But how, the young poet wonders, does one convey the feel of emotion in language? Some of his first experiments at expressive emotionality fail utterly. Distressed by Chatterton's suicide at eighteen, Keats tries, unsuccessfully, to symbolize his pity by spastic exclamatory utterance:

> O Chatterton! how very sad thy fate!
> Dear child of sorrow! son of misery!
> How soon the film of death obscur'd that eye,
> Whence genius wildly flashed, and high debate!
> How soon that voice, majestic and elate,
> Melted in dying murmurs! Oh! how nigh
> Was night to thy fair morning!
> (*To Chatterton*, 1815)

The seven exclamation marks in as many lines surely suggest Keats's strong response to Chatterton's "sad fate," but no syntactic means occurs to him other than the exclamatory, and no semantic means other than the repetition of synonyms—*sad, sorrow, misery*. The early sonnets exhibit many such outbursts; in some, Keats varies the exclamation points with question marks, as in the rhetorical attitude struck about female beauty:

> Ah! who can e'er forget so fair a being?
> Who can forget her half retiring sweets?
> God! she is like a milk-white lamb that bleats
> For man's protection.
> (*Ah, who can e'er forget*, 1815–1816)

And these are among the sonnets Keats decided to *publish*, from which we can infer that there were worse ones, perhaps destroyed or never even committed to paper. As he wrote in 1816 to Charles Cowden Clarke, "I have coppied out a sheet or two of Verses which I composed some time ago, and find so much to blame in them that the best part will go into the fire" (L, I, 113).

Keats's taste, at this point, is still so uncertain that he can produce, on the very same occasion, two sonnets of which one is good and the other bad. We are thereby led to ask what misstep leads astray the "false" twin. In the *Poems* of 1817, he published two sonnets written (according to Charles Cowden Clarke) close together, both of which recount his emotions as he walks home from an evening at Leigh Hunt's cottage. *On Leaving Some Friends at an Early Hour* is embarrassing in its adoption of images from conventional Christianity (an ideological system in which Keats has no spiritual or emotional investment). Inspired by his evening with Hunt, Keats desires (he says) to write poetry of a sort possible only to the angels:

> Give me a golden pen, and let me lean
>   On heap'd up flowers, in regions clear, and far;
>   Bring me a tablet whiter than a star,
> Or hand of hymning angel, when 'tis seen
> The silver strings of heavenly harp atween:
>   And let there glide by many a pearly car,
>   Pink robes, and wavy hair, and diamond jar,
> And half discovered wings.
>   (*On Leaving Some Friends at an Early Hour*,
>   October/November 1816)

This sonnet is written, culturally speaking, on automatic pilot, as the poet borrows Christian diction familiar to nineteenth-century readers in order to illustrate the "height" for which his spirit is "contending" in its compositorial enthusiasm. The young poet endangers his art by trying to convey his inner aspiration in terms familiar to his audience rather than in terms authentic to himself.

The inept *On Leaving Some Friends* sprang from the same occasion as *Keen, fitful gusts are whisp'ring here and there,* a sonnet that is intensely personal both in its opening natural detail and in its closing literary evocations:

> Keen, fitful gusts are whisp'ring here and there
>> Among the bushes half leafless, and dry;
>> The stars look very cold about the sky,
> And I have many miles on foot to fare.
> Yet feel I little of the cool bleak air,
>> Or of the dead leaves rustling drearily,
>> Or of those silver lamps that burn on high,
> Or of the distance from home's pleasant lair:
> For I am brimfull of the friendliness
>> That in a little cottage I have found;
> Of fair-hair'd Milton's eloquent distress,
>> And all his love for gentle Lycid drown'd;
> Of lovely Laura in her light green dress,
>> And faithful Petrarch gloriously crown'd.

There are some lapses here: the "silver lamps that burn on high" come from the general stock of the poetic warehouse, and a human home, for rhyme's sake, is awkwardly referred to as a *lair* (although Keats tries to attenuate the usual connection of this word to poverty or predators by attaching the mitigating *pleasant*). There is a degree of deleted intellectuality, too, in the poem: Keats has suppressed both Milton's excoriation in *Lycidas* of the corrupt clergy and Petrarch's Christian remorse. For this very reason, though, we feel that we are hearing what an ardent young poet might be likely to remember of *Lycidas* and the *Canzoniere*.

Keats's distinctive twinned adjectives in such phrases as *keen, fitful* gusts, *half-leafless and dry* bushes, and *cool bleak* air suggest an effort at a complex accuracy. These markedly original modifiers, engaging two senses at once, are a far cry from the other sonnet's conventional single adjectives: *silver* strings, *pink* robes, *wavy* hair, and a *hymning* angel. In the "angelic" sonnet, there is no discoverable progression or alteration of thought, no fruitful use of the binary nature of the sonnet form: the octave wants a golden pen and the company of angels, and the sestet merely reiterates those desires, wanting to use the pen to "write down a line of glorious tone" and acknowledging that it is not good "to be alone." *Keen, fitful gusts,* by contrast, fulfills the intrinsic duality of the Petrarchan sonnet in moving backwards in time from the cold outdoor octave to the warm indoor sestet, where both long-vanished characters in poems and the dead authors of those poems take on life.

The sestet-adjectives of *Keen, fitful gusts* are not double but single, because they deal not with contending personal perceptions, as the octave-adjectives do, but with received and known tradition: they tell of the aesthetic and ethical nature of literature. Keats's predecessor-poets are humanly evoked in such characterizing epithets as *fair-hair'd* Milton and *faithful* Petrarch—persons respectively beautiful and constant: Milton possesses both eloquence (an aesthetic quality) and love of his dead friend (a moral quality); and Petrarch exhibits both fidelity (a moral quality) and—in being crowned with Apollo's bays—aesthetic success. The persons whom the poets love are characterized by pastoral names and stereotypical ethical or aesthetic adjectives (*gentle Lycid* and *lovely Laura*). The words *friendliness, fair-hair'd,* and *faithful* make a meaningful alliterative chain linking the social cottage, the personal beauty of a precursor-poet, and the moral claim of strong emotions; and the individual affections memorialized in the literature of the past—Milton's friendship, Petrarch's love—find their analogue in the contemporary social friendliness of the sheltering cottage. The sensuous appeal of Milton's and Petrarch's poetry is recalled in the sonic liquidity and aesthetic innocence of the *berceuse* conveyed by the recurrently-rhyming—*cdcdcd*—and rhythmically-lulling sestet: Keats is "brimfull" "Of fair-hair'd Milton's eloquent distress, / And all his love for gentle Lycid drown'd; / Of lovely Laura in her light green dress, / And faithful Petrarch gloriously crown'd." (It is not surprising that the Keats in love with such liquid harmonies would at first resist the harsher and fiercer sonorities of *Lear*.)

Why—when he was able to compose the fine and touching sonnet *Keen, fitful gusts*—would Keats write *On Leaving Some Friends* (with its inauthentic Christianity), except that he was hoping to please a reading public stocked with ready-made responses to angels with pink robes and wavy hair? Keats may have feared that general readers would not be moved by lines about how cold the stars looked to him or about literary exchange within a friend's cottage. Because Keats's own generosity of spirit made him instinctively reach out to his addressees—his brothers, Hunt, Reynolds, Haydon—he must have wished to create links with eventual readers outside his intimate acquaintance. Violating his own free-thinking convictions by making reference to Christian symbols was not, however, the way to reach an audience. He needed to find experiences authentic to himself but neither eccentric or private, and to evoke them in images to which others could respond.

Keats accomplishes such a potential sharing of common feeling when, departing from simple replication of literary content (*lovely Laura* and *faithful Petrarch*), he describes the effect of reading Homer—not merely by mentioning *deep-brow'd Homer* (in the manner of *fair-hair'd Milton*) but by finding three figures recognizable to an ordinary audience: the seasoned traveler sailing "round many western islands," the astronomer ("some watcher of the skies"), and the explorer ("stout Cortez"). These figures bring the felt exaltation of literary discovery home to any reader. Keats, not possessing Greek, knows what it is to be ignorant: he himself, before reading Chapman, hadn't been able to sense the poetry of Homer. The exalted passage from ignorance to knowledge climaxing in the sestet's "wild surmise" of further exploration is assumed to be one that any reader will have analogously undergone. And in making this link with common experience, Keats writes the sonnet in which all his early practice culminates:

On First Looking into Chapman's Homer

Much have I travell'd in the realms of gold,
    And many goodly states and kingdoms seen;
    Round many western islands have I been
Which bards in fealty to Apollo hold.
Oft of one wide expanse had I been told
    That deep-brow'd Homer ruled as his demesne;
    Yet did I never breathe its pure serene
Till I heard Chapman speak out loud and bold:
Then felt I like some watcher of the skies
    When a new planet swims into his ken;
Or like stout Cortez when with eagle eyes
    He star'd at the Pacific—and all his men
Look'd at each other with a wild surmise—
    Silent, upon a peak in Darien.
        (October 1816)[5]

The first thing that may strike us as a sign of structural mastery in this two-sentence sonnet is Keats's firm syntactic chain of carefully delineated tenses organizing the octave: "Much *have I* travell'd," "Round . . . islands *have I* been," "Oft . . . *had I* been told," "Yet never *did I* breathe," "Till *I heard* Chapman." The suspense of the steady narrative progress through present-perfect and pluperfect forms causes the simple preterite of "Till I *heard*" strike on the ear as if a voice had spoken aloud: and the change in aspect from the visual to the auditory creates a parallel impact. The strategic absence of a concessive in the first line (such as "*Though* I had travell'd in the realms of gold") causes the first quatrain, framed in ceremonious end-stopped lines, to seem one of ripe, even complacent, Odyssean wisdom, in no danger of being surpassed: "Much have I travell'd . . . And many goodly states and kingdoms seen." Suspense enters with the mention of a rumored "wide expanse" which is ruled by Homer but which is surprisingly, as yet, unknown to the richly-traveled speaker. Keats's deliberately vague descriptive phrase *wide expanse* provokes implicit questions: Is this "expanse" an island, a state, a kingdom? How big is "wide"? Can one go there? What does it feel like to arrive there?

The sestet's preterite consequent—"Then *felt I*"—issues in the two similes that replace the octave's metaphor of the sea-voyager through the known world. Once we have seen the first simile—that of the watcher of the skies perceiving a new planet—we might ask: "Why does the poem not end here? Why is a supplementary simile—that of 'stout Cortez . . . and all his men'—necessary?" If Keats had been satisfied with the adequacy of the astronomer, he could easily have elaborated that simile through four more lines. The *or* that introduces Keats's subsequent, substitutive simile—"*Or* like stout Cortez"—together with the replacement of the single watcher by the plural company of Cortez "and all his men" suggests that there was something incomplete about the earlier image of the astronomer. "Then felt I like—" "Like this," Keats says, and then corrects himself—"Or [rather] [more] like that." Keats's successive similes show him searching for a satisfyingly accurate rendering of the contour of his feelings. (Simile, unlike metaphor, always implies provisionality.)

It is our sense of Keats's active search for the right simile—"What is reading Chapman's *Homer* like?"—that organizes our response to his sestet. There was no active thinking necessary to summon angels with pink robes or even to recall Petrarch and Laura. Suddenly we discover, in the sestet of *Chapman's Homer,* the sinewy Keats of the *Letters*—someone actively wrestling with experience, sorting it and charting it. The complete self-forgetfulness of the sestet—as the hitherto prominent "I" disappears entirely as a voiced pronoun after "Then felt I"—reflects Keats's plunge into a treasury of generally available, rather than topically personal, life-images. As we see him first inventing, then dropping, the astronomer, we realize that this figure now seems to him too passive, too isolated, too impotent. The astronomer, alone in his prolonged and attentive vigil, does nothing physically active to gain his new knowledge: it is the planet, by its own energy, that "swims" into his ken. And, crucially, the astronomer cannot visit the "wide expanse" he beholds: it is inaccessible. More-over, the observatory experience is a solitary one: no one else is pres-ent as the watcher views the planet. These inadequacies of reference press Keats on to a second, more satisfactory representation of his new knowledge—a discovery that differs from his earlier acquisitions not in degree but in kind. As "stout Cortez" stares at the Pacific, the "expanse" of Homer's poetry is shown to be not a land-mass—an is-land or a state comparable to those the seasoned traveler has already seen—but rather an entire ocean offering innumerable new shores and islands for future exploration. Moreover, "Cortez" makes the dis-covery in the company of "all his men," just as Keats made his discov-ery of Homer not only through the society of those who had "oft" told him about Homer, but also with the aid of Chapman, the cul-tural mediator of an ancient text written in a foreign tongue. One makes literary discoveries not alone, but as a member of a trans-historical cultural company of writers, readers, and translators.

Remembering the opening ceremonious cadence of the much-traveled speaker of the octave, we are struck not only by the persis-tence of that undisturbed rhythm in the relatively unexcited pace of the two lines about the watcher of the skies, but also by the disrup-tion of that placidity of rhythm in the subsequent, more accurate rendition of a grander—but nonetheless humanly explorable—plane of discovery. Keats opens his vista of a new world with three ac-cented syllables containing strong vowels—"Or *like stout Cortez*"— and then, as astonishment at last finds its rhythmic equivalent, he unsettles the last three lines by a dash, a strong enjambment, another dash, and a rare first-foot comma.

The young Keats has learned, we see, to write a "perfect" Petrarchan sonnet, one that readers—to borrow a phrase from Mil-ton—have not willingly let die. If the chief signs of poetic maturity include an invention of sharable symbols, the fit of syntax to narra-tive, the intellectual adequacy of image to experience, and a rhythmi-cally convincing personal voice, then we can say that in October 1816, as he writes this sonnet, Keats has become mature.

The sestet of this sonnet rhymes in the same way—*cdcdcd*—as that of *Keen, fitful gusts,* but the broken syntax here is far from the child-like, if devoted, music representing "gentle Lycid" and "lovely Laura." Keats's literary appetite has moved from the beautiful to the arduous and the ardent, to a willingness to invoke and convey force rather than loveliness or pathos. Laura and Lycid remain in the realm of the beautiful; but "stout Cortez," as everyone has remarked, belongs to the epic sublime. The three words that most evoke the sublime in this sonnet are *eagle, star'd,* and *wild.* Keats had originally written *wond'ring eyes,* eyes which could still belong to the mild plane of pastoral. By revising the adjective to *eagle,* he leaves the ground behind and rises to the heavens, not on eagle wings, but by the eagle's piercing sight.[6] We might have expected Cortez to *look* (by analogy to the title's *looking into* and the men's *look'd at*) but instead (and unbeautifully) Cortez fiercely *stare[s],* a word of riveted fixation rather than of traveled contemplation or telescopic wonder. And although Cortez's men look at each other, they do so with a *wild* surmise, not a merely curious or satisfied one.

The young Keats can't, of course, maintain a sure grasp on the sublime. The "angelic" sonnet—a poem composed *after* the one on Chapman's Homer—betrays, as we've seen, a concession to sentimental Christian iconography. Still, in having dared the fierce and ambitious image of Cortez, Keats has readied himself for further searches in epic areas—those that will ultimately lead to the internal, but historical, tragic theater of the Titaness Moneta in *The Fall of Hyperion.* Her contemplation of human grief will displace heroic masculine achievement as the site of the Keatsian sublime. As early as 1816 (but not in a sonnet) Keats had foreseen, and even acquiesced in, a commitment to tragedy, when for a brief three and a half lines in *Sleep and Poetry* (ll. 122–125) he glimpsed his future:

> And can I ever bid these joys farewell?
> Yes, I must pass them for a nobler life,
> Where I may find the agonies, the strife
> Of human hearts.

We'll come in a moment to Keats's 1818 sonnet announcing his turn toward the tragic, but first I want to point out a second form of early sonnet-mastery that is as characteristic of Keats, in its own way, as his reach to the sublime in *Chapman's Homer*. I am referring to Keats's achievement, in some early sonnets, of a complex union—neither tragic nor comic—of intimacy, detached objectivity, and lightness of touch (qualities we have already seen in Milton's *L'Allegro*). Such aspects appear in the double adjectives of *Keen, fitful gusts,* but they achieve their early Keatsian summit in the little sonnet *On the Grasshopper and Cricket,* written in light-hearted competition with Leigh Hunt.[7]

Yeats once said that "gradual time's last gift" was "a written speech / Full of high laughter, loveliness and ease" *(Upon a House Shaken by the Land Agitation). On the Grasshopper and Cricket* exhibits that ultimate gift. Somber by the dread that is its backdrop (voiced in the premonitory words *dead* and *ceasing*), it is made light by its octave of summer luxury. Grave (in the sestet) by the cold words *lone* and *winter* and *silence,* it is made humorous by the sprightly verb *shrills* and the unliterary *stove.* Written in a few brief minutes, it shows perfect and effortless grace. Only a poet who had practiced the form of the sonnet until it became second nature—this is Keats's twenty-sixth surviving sonnet—could spontaneously throw off *On the Grasshopper and Cricket.* But Hunt, too, had written sonnets with great frequency, and his sonnet fails. Hunt's is a sonnet of the fancy, and Keats's is a sonnet of the imagination.

On the Grasshopper and Cricket was composed on December 30, in the dead of winter, the time of silent frost and of *Il Penseroso*'s cricket on the hearth. But Keats doesn't begin with the frost and the cricket, any more than he'll begin the autumn ode with the stubble-plains that inspired it. Instead, his reparatory imagination, in which the seasonal cycle is always hovering, speeds forward from deprivation to plenitude; and just as he'll begin *To Autumn* with the loaded apple trees and overbrimming honeycombs of late summer, so he begins this sonnet, haunted by the potential death of song, with the comic hops of the irrepressible Grasshopper:

On the Grasshopper and Cricket

The poetry of earth is never dead:
   When all the birds are faint with the hot sun,
   And hide in cooling trees, a voice will run
From hedge to hedge about the new-mown mead;
That is the Grasshopper's—he takes the lead
   In summer luxury,—he has never done
With his delights; for when tired out with fun
He rests at ease beneath some pleasant weed.

Keats's receptive absorption of natural phenomena sometimes seemed to him to signify indolence or passivity. But when it didn't induce guilt, it gave acute enjoyment, nowhere more visible than in this lightly sketched sonnet, where Keats's aesthetic maturity is shown by the absence of any straining after either largeness or coyness of effect. *On the Grasshopper* is, however mutedly, a poem facing terminal loss. The speaker has noticed, with apprehension, that the dawn chorus of birds has fallen silent, because it is high noon at high summer and the birds are hiding in "cooling trees." A voice within him says, apprehensively, "The poetry of earth has died." Searching round to rebut that voice, the poet declares, "No: noon has its music too: the birds may be silent, but I hear the grasshopper's song."

The conspicuous enjambments of lines 3–4, 5–6, 6–7, and even 7–8 mimic the successive leaps of the grasshopper's springy travels. Keats has by now learned how to make syntax mimic physical motion, so that the phrasal movements of the sonnet wonderfully enact their own observations. The motion tracked in the octave—after the initial proposition rebutting Keats's presentiment that the poetry of earth might indeed be able to die—is that of the grasshopper's hopping from hedge to hedge as he sings. Pulled by enjambment, we follow his hops in three successive voicings, followed by a fourth allowing him to rest: "That is the Grasshopper's" [hop]—"he takes the lead / In summer luxury" [hop]—"he has never done / With his delights" [hop]—"for when tired out with fun / He rests." The hedge-hopping grasshopper moves horizontally, so the poet must afford him places to hop to. Keats therefore goes to work stationing both the planar and vertical elements of the landscape: he mentions trees, hedges, a new-mown mead, and a "pleasant" weed. By the end of the octave, each level of height has been established, from the floor of the mown meadow through the small verticality of a weed, to the higher reach of hedges, all of these lying below the higher trees, the home of the silent birds. (This compact three-dimensional scene-sketching will reach its imaginative perfection in the creation of the virtual bower in the *Nightingale* ode, where the speaker, unable to see in darkness, "guesses" each element surrounding him.) As we "run / From hedge to hedge" with the grasshopper, we intuit the successive loci of the poetry of earth as the grasshopper's lively voice constitutes them by its emergence, and we participate in Keats's gratitude that even when the birds fall silent the summer season has an intermittent voice, hitherto unnoticed, to offer the ear.

The poet repeats his initial rebuttal in a different form in the sestet, taking full advantage of the binary form offered by the Petrarchan sonnet, but playing with it. The opening line of the sestet seems merely to repeat the opening line of the octave, and we imagine that the sestet will be nothing more than a restating of the octave. Yet Keats uses the sestet powerfully, showing that the two apparently identical propositions rebut two very different threats. He had previously insisted that "The poetry of earth is never dead" in answer to the sinister inner interlocutor who has asserted that the summer silence means that the poetry of earth is now dead. The interlocutor now returns, but this time to rebut the cheerful octave with a second gloomy assertion resembling his first ("is dead") but extending it over time (to "is ceasing"): "Well, even if the poetry of earth is not yet *entirely* dead, it is in the *process* of ceasing; when winter arrives there will be no songs, whether of birds or of grasshoppers." "The poetry of earth is ceasing never"—Keats's vigorous refutation of this second implied warning—is embodied in a second natural creature: the Miltonic cricket on the hearth. It is now winter; we are indoors; heat comes not from the natural sun, not even from a visible fire, but from the modern and prosaic stove; and the first enjambment in this part of the poem represents not the hops of a running summer voice but the stealth of a silence far more deathly than the temporary hush of the birds:

> The poetry of earth is ceasing never:
>> On a lone winter evening, when the frost
>>> Has wrought a silence, from the stove there shrills
> The Cricket's song.

Keats's presentation of the cricket is a suspended one, as he reserves the grammatical subject of the second clause, *the Cricket's song,* to the end. And by contrast to the octave's narrative, which takes place in a generalized season, the sestet offers a much briefer narrative, that of a single winter evening:

> On a lone
>> winter   the Cricket's song.
>>> evening,   there shrills
>>>> when the frost   from the stove
>>> has wrought a silence,

The syntax descends, word by word, to a nadir of cold silence, broken magically by the unexpected trill of the Cricket. This would be reason enough for relief, but the poem offers more than relief; it offers joy. The Cricket's song is made to be unceasing by constantly increasing not in volume or frequency but in "warmth": it is itself the spiritual heat-source of the winter room, just as the stove is the physical heat-source.

As if defending itself against the nay-saying of its invisible interlocutor, the poem in its octave had turned to gaiety and fancifulness as adornments to its calendrical objectivity; it had allowed itself the pleasant anthropomorphizing fictions that the birds are "faint" and that the grasshopper is "tired out with fun." But as fear returns to the poet, the sestet departs from fancifulness and modulates into gravity. Even if at one select summer moment one hears the grasshopper, and at another select winter moment one hears the cricket, these isolated instances by themselves can't prove the absolute *never* of the poet's two forceful rebuttals. Even the ever-amplifying warmth of the Cricket's song doesn't prove the unbreakable continuity of nature's music, reassuring though the progressive verb *increasing* and Keats's assertive *ever* (rhyming in defiant positivity against the rebutting *never*) may be. We've been promised, by the two propositions, a perpetual and unbroken constancy in the poetry of earth that we haven't yet reached. We've seen two individual vignettes of beatitude, but nothing that joins them.

It is only at the last moment, as we become intimate with the sweet drowsiness of the youthful Keatsian imagination (which is nonetheless objectively depicted as belonging to a third-person *one*), that we find the uninterrupted circle of beatitude:

> from the stove there shrills
> The Cricket's song, in warmth increasing ever,
> And seems to one in drowsiness half lost,
> The Grasshopper's among some grassy hills.

The objectivity of knowledge claimed by the propositional rebuttals opening both octave and sestet is not disturbed by this fantasy, so carefully pointed out as fantasy by *seems, drowsiness,* and *half lost.* This is a self-aware fancy, since the listener is only "half" lost; but it is a viable one because the unbroken circle of beatitude is, after all, a logical extrapolation—to every moment of the year—of the two already-bestowed revelations of music vanquishing silence, the summer one and the winter one. It is imagination—positing a natural identity of the two seasonal revelations—that closes the circle. The magical effect by which the phrase *grassy hills* repeats the sound of *Grasshopper* becomes the linguistic sign of the mellifluous continuability of the winter song into the summer one. The alliterative iteration makes—to the listener's dreamy solace—every moment in the year one of potential natural song. If it were not the July grasshopper, it could be the August bees; if it were not the December cricket, it could be the March whistle of the redbreast. The moral is one of faith and vigilance: listen and ye shall hear. But such a moral can never be pointed by objective attentiveness alone: it is the imagination and its dream that perform the extrapolatory revelation.

As we have seen, Keats has found a convincing, secular, and share-able sublime in *Chapman's Homer,* and a firm natural objectivity that allows room for fantasy, humor, and imagination in *On the Grass-hopper and Cricket.* But what has been haunting him, as he said in *Sleep and Poetry,* is tragedy, which he has so far avoided in his son-nets. How can he incorporate the tragic into the sonnet? His ac-knowledgment of agony and strife appears in sonnet form only after the publication of the *Poems* of 1817. This turning point of his lyric theory comes on the 22nd of January, 1818, when he composes a sonnet on *King Lear.* In a letter written on the same day to Benjamin Bailey, he mentions in a single breath his brother Tom's continuing hemorrhages and the decision to embark on the sonnet: "My Brother Tom is getting stronger but his spitting of blood continues—I sat down to read King Lear yesterday and felt the greatness of the thing up to the writing of a Sonnet preparatory thereto" (L, I, 212). Tom's illness—he would die within the year—was bound to compel Keats's imagination toward tragedy; or perhaps Tom's plight reanimated in Keats memories of their mother's death that enabled the admission of a tragic sense present since his boyhood but long repressed in his verse. On the same day as he writes to Bailey, he sends a letter to his brothers, in which he mentions *King Lear* in the context of a "gradual ripening" of his "intellectual powers":

I think a little change has taken place in my intellect lately—I cannot bear to be uninterested or unemployed, I, who for so long a time, have been addicted to passiveness. Nothing is finer for the purposes of great productions, than a very gradual rip-ening of the intellectual powers—As an instance of this—ob-serve—I sat down yesterday to read King Lear once again the

thing appeared to demand the prologue of a Sonnet, I wrote it
& began to read. (L, I, 214)

The sonnet on *Lear* marks the exact moment of Keats's intellectual
break with the Romance mode, the mode from which most of his
earlier sonnets had sprung. On the wintry day of 22 January 1818,
Keats is prompted, by his purposeful intent to reread *Lear*, to look
back with hindsight at the state of mind in which he wrote his
Petrarchan sonnets. *On Sitting Down to Read King Lear Once Again*,
a hybrid sonnet, aims its address successively toward two different
muses. In the Petrarchan octave, Keats addresses the female muse of
Spenserian Romance, bidding her adieu (in one of those many Keats-
ian adieux that culminate in the odes):[8]

> O golden-tongued Romance, with serene lute!
> Fair plumèd syren, queen of far-away!
> Leave melodizing on this wintry day,
> Shut up thine olden pages, and be mute.
> Adieu!

Keats here dismisses serenity, Faeryland, and the Muse in her female,
eroticized form. He excuses his turn away from Romance with the
explanation that he intends, for a second time, to confront the expe-
rience of reading *King Lear*—that play in which there is no justice,
only suffering and its stricken obverse, joy. In the sonnet on Chap-
man, reading Homer was represented by similes of far cosmic see-
ing and superb oceanic finding; but the reading of Shakespearean
tragedy demands of Keats not provisional similes but permanent
metaphors. In the terrifying first of these, he declares that he must
"burn through" the play's "fierce dispute / Betwixt damnation and
impassion'd clay"; and we learn later in the poem that he expects to
be "consumèd" in the mimetic fire of that reading. Keats's first read-
ing of *King Lear*, we gather, had been a reluctant one; resisting its an-
guish, he could not yield himself wholly to its searing power. Now, he
resolves to submit himself voluntarily to the pyre. But his second

metaphor remembers that the play is not only an ethical document, a fierce mimesis of racked life; it is also an aesthetic object that gives exquisite sensation, a bitter-sweet fruit whose taste he must humbly "assay." Using a chiasmus (an *abba* semantic positioning), which is always the figure of forethought, of conscious arrangement (by contrast to the more "natural" *abab* linearity of the stream of consciousness), Keats balances the two metaphorical actions—respectively moral and aesthetic—that he must undertake on confronting the play. We see, in the chiasmus, *noun-verb-verb-noun:* the *dispute* that he must *burn through,* and the *assay* of its *bitter-sweet fruit* :

> Adieu! for, once again, the fierce dispute
> > Betwixt damnation and impassion'd clay
> > Must I burn through: once more humbly assay
> The bitter-sweet of this Shaksperean fruit.

To the Petrarchan octave bidding farewell to the female muse of Romance, Keats now appends a sestet that is rhymed according to the Shakespearean model, because it is addressed to the male muse he has newly adopted: Shakespeare, the King not of far-away but of the near at hand—Albion, Lear's and Keats's England. Surprisingly, there is a second (and plural, and perhaps implicitly female) addressee as well, the "clouds of Albion" who are characterized (with an allusion to the "onlie begetter" of Shakespeare's *Sonnets*) as the "Begetters of our deep eternal theme." These clouds (like their counterparts in the odes on Indolence and on Melancholy) seem to stand for the transcendent and ever-nascent sorrow behind the eternal theme of tragedy; they breed perpetual tears. Earlier, reading had seemed to Keats comparable to exotic traveling in Grecian isles and uncharted continents, but now it becomes—in positive metaphor, rather than speculative simile—an uncertain wandering on Keats's inherited native ground, the primal oak forest of Lear's Druidic Britain:

> Chief Poet! and ye clouds of Albion,
> > Begetters of our deep eternal theme!

> When through the old oak forest I am gone,
> Let me not wander in a barren dream.

Fearing to be lost, like an erring Spenserian character, in the forest of tragic apprehension, Keats hopes that something good will come from his purposeful rejection of Romance, the genre that had been the most congenial to his idealizing youthful imagination. The whole of the 1818 *Endymion* had been a defense of Romance; its very subtitle was *A Romance*. What can replace Romance and its fair plumes? Can the fire-consumèd creature rise on different pinions?

> But, when I am consumèd in the fire,
> Give me new phoenix wings to fly at my desire.

(We recall that the phoenix of Shakespeare's *The Phoenix and the Turtle* is male, and is therefore available to Keats as a self-image.) In spite of its commitment to Shakespearean tragedy, *On Sitting Down to Read King Lear Once Again* is identifiable as an "early" poem because Keats still desires wings: he hasn't yet "moulted," hasn't given up wings for "patient sublunary legs" (To J. H. Reynolds, 11 July 1819: L, II, 128). Nonetheless, the poem acknowledges the inevitability of tragic experience, an acknowledgment thematically symbolized by the sonnet's explicit turn from Spenserian Romance to Shakespearean tragedy, and formally symbolized by the turn from a Petrarchan octave to a Shakespearean sestet.

Has the poet then absolutely repudiated Spenser's melodizing and the Petrarchan lute in his vow to taste the Shakespearean fruit, enter the Shakespearean forest, and burn in the Shakespearean fire? (By alliteration, Keats links the three words *fruit, forest,* and *fire* in a single Shakespearean cluster.) Keats's generosity of spirit toward his earlier poetic "Presiders" would forbid such a gesture of total exclusion. Petrarch, therefore, is granted the octave-rhymes; and, although Keats *rhymes* his sestet according to Shakespeare, he ends it with a line that *scans* according to Spenser. The hexameter that closes the sonnet—"Give me new phoenix wings / to fly at my desire"—looks back in homage to the hexameters with which Spenser ends his stanzas in *The Faerie Queene.*[9]

We may take this 1818 sonnet on *Lear* as Keats's retrospective critique of his own early poems, including the Petrarchan sonnets. They looked to the far-away, and to serene melodizing, and to the dream-idealizations of Romance; they admitted neither dispute nor damnation nor fire; they did not want to see human beings as "clay," even if "impassioned clay." Their fruit was sweet rather than "bitter-sweet"; they did not demand of their reader that he be consumed in entering their precincts. They chose habitable bowers or visionary peaks rather than forests of potential error. Keats's self-criticisms implicit in the sonnet on *Lear,* resembling those in his original Preface to *Endymion,* are harsh ones, but they are justified as he recognizes—in the presence of his dying brother Tom—the manifest discrepancy between his early knowledge of tragedy (in the premature deaths of his parents and baby brother Edward and the 1814 death of his beloved grandmother, who, when his mother left for a second marriage, raised him) and the willed exclusion of tragic events and emotions from most of his work before 1817. When we read the youthful Petrarchan sonnets, we must be aware of how intent they are on suppressing everything that Keats already bitterly knew of fatal accident, fatal illness, premature death, and permanent loss.

Keats will write greater poems than the 1817 sonnets, and his apprenticeship in the sonnet will go on to bolder formal explorations as he writes not only such powerful Shakespearean sonnets as *Bright star,* but also his brilliant irregular sonnets *To Sleep* and *If by dull rhymes.* What Wallace Stevens said about the writing of an extended poem—that it was like a prolonged serenade to a señorita, that all sorts of favors would drop from it—can equally be said of a long apprenticeship to a genre. In his early practice of the sonnet between 1814 and 1817, Keats grew up with respect to language, syntax, rhythm, rhyme, and architectonic form, finding boldness with Cortez and lightness with the grasshopper, locating distinctive adjectives for natural observation and persuasive tones for the intimacy of social warmth, using the binary form of the sonnet to good purpose (outdoors versus indoors, the known versus the new). Moreover, since he could learn from his mistakes, he found out that borrowing conventional symbols (whether patriotic, as in *To Kosciusko,* or religious, as in *On Leaving Some Friends*) was an impediment to truth of utterance. Most of all, he exercised a Shakespearean ardor in hunting down, by simile and metaphor, the fictive correlatives adequate to the particulars of his experience. And he found the metrical and syntactical means to match the dulcet rhythm of lovely Laura, the abrupt rhythm of Darien discovery, the buoyant rhythm of a grasshopper's hops, the chiastic rhythm of *Lear's* double moral and aesthetic demand. Through his work on the early Petrarchan sonnets, he became the Keats we know. Another young poet might have remained content with the "perfect" sonnet on Homer. Keats's depth of heart and mind required that he go on to enter, within a year, the burning nest of the Phoenix to write the sonnet of Shakespearean fruit, and forest, and fire.

Appendix: Sonnets Composed by Keats

Dating and page numbers are from *The Poems of John Keats,* ed. Jack Stillinger (Harvard University Press, 1978).

Sonnet Types, Classified by Rhyme-Scheme

In the case of a longer line, I specify the number of feet in subscript after the affected line number: e.g., 14_6 indicates a final hexameter. Rhyme schemes are in standard type. I underline rhyme *units* such as quatrains or tercets or couplets as they occur in Keats's octaves and sestets. They help to identify the differing components of the Keatsian sestet.

REGULAR TYPES

P = Petrarchan: abba abba octave, plus sestet. Nine types, classified by the form of the sestet.

40 sonnets (1814–1818) begin with a Petrarchan octave. Their sestet-types are as follows:

P_1 = cde cde (two rhyming tercets).
  6 sonnets: #10, 12, 19, 26, 30, 38 (1815–1817)

P_2 = Shakespearean quatrain, plus ?

  P_{2a} = cdcd cd (Shakespearean quatrain plus continued rhyme)
    22 sonnets: #2, 3, 4, 5, 6, 7, 8, 11, 17, 18, 20, 21, 23, 28, 29, 32, 33, 34, 36, 39, 43, 51 (1814–1818)
  P_{2a+} = cdcd cd with 14_6
    1 sonnet: #13 ["To a Friend"] (1816)

P_{2a-} = cdcd [c-]d: shortened 5th line, unrhymed
  1 sonnet: #22 ["Great spirits "] (1817)
P_{2b} = cdcd dc (Shakespearean quatrain plus reversed rhyme)
  1 sonnet: #25 ["Written in Disgust"] (1816)

P_3 = Petrarchan quatrain, plus ?
  P_{3a} = cddc dc (Petrarchan quatrain plus reversed rhyme)
    2 sonnets: #9 ["O Solitude"] (1815),
                #16 ["How many bards"] (1816)
  P_{3b} = cddc ee (Petrarchan quatrain plus Shakespearean couplet)
    1 sonnet: #31 ["This pleasant tale"] (1817)

P_4 = c dede c (bracketed quatrain)
  4 sonnets: #14, #35, #37 (1817), #50 (1818)

P_5 = (sestet contains no quatrain)
  2 sonnets: #24 ["To Kosciusko"} (1816) [cdedce),
              #27 ["After dark vapours"] (1817) [cdefdf]
Total Petrarchan: 40

S = **Shakespearean** (three alternately-rhymed quatrains plus couplet)
  S: Regular Shakespearean sonnet
    14 sonnets: #41, 42, 44, 45, 47, 48, 49, 52, 53,
        56, 58, 60, 63, 64 (1818–1819)
  S^+: Shakespearean sonnet with 14_6
    1 sonnet: #57["As Hermes once"] (1819)
                                        Total Shakespearean: 15
                          TOTAL OF REGULAR SONNETS: 55

ANOMALOUS TYPES

H = **Hybrid.** Three types:

  H_P = Petrarchan octave with Shakespearean sestet [cdcd ee]:
    2 sonnets: #15 ["To My Brother George"] (1816),
                #53 ["Of late two dainties"] (1818)

H_{P+} = Petrarchan octave with Shakespearean sestet having 14_6:
   1 sonnet: #40 ["On sitting down to read"] (1818)

H_{s++} = Shakespearean octave with Petrarchan sestet [dd ed ee]
   having 9_7 and 14_6.
   1 sonnet: #1 ["On Peace"] (1814)

Total Hybrid: 4

I = **Irregularly rhymed sonnet.** Three types:
   3 sonnets:
      #59 ["To Sleep] (1819):
         Shakespearean octave with sestet bc efef
      #61 ["How fever'd is the man"] (1819):
         Shakespearean octave with sestet efe gg f
      #62 ["If by dull rhymes"] (1819):
         abc ab(d)c abc dede (tercets, quatrain)

U = **Unrhymed sonnet:**
   1 sonnet: #46 ["O thou whose face hath felt the Winter's wind"]
      (1818)

D = **Douzain** reduced in translation from French sonnet:
   1 sonnet: #55 ["Nature withheld Cassandra in the skies"] (1818)

Total Other: 5

TOTAL ANOMALOUS: 9

GRAND TOTAL, REGULAR AND ANOMALOUS: 64

Sonnets Written by Keats, with Dates of Composition and of First Publication

Key to Annotations:

* = Published in *Poems 1817*. 21 sonnets. Roman numerals indicate the number of the sonnet in the group entitled "Sonnets" in *Poems 1817*. In addition to those 17 sonnets, *1817* contains a dedicatory sonnet and a poem (listed under "Poems") beginning "Woman! when I behold thee": this consists of three stanzas, each of which is a Petrarchan sonnet. I count this, for the purpose of this table, as three sonnets.

* — = Magazine publication before *Poems 1817,* but not included in that volume: 2 sonnets: "After dark vapours" and "This pleasant tale."

** = Magazine publication after *Poems 1817* (Keats published no sonnets in *Poems 1820*): 6 sonnets.

Italics = Unpublished sonnets composed pre-*1817:* 9 sonnets.

Numbers in parentheses refer to page numbers in Stillinger's *Poems.*

Total number of sonnets written before publication of *Poems 1817* = 32
Total number of sonnets written after publication of *Poems 1817* = 32
Total number of sonnets composed by Keats = 64

Sonnets Written Before *Poems 1817*

1. *On Peace* (28)
   [? April 1814 (publ. 1905)]
   H_{s++}: Hybrid: S octave, P sestet (dd ed ee), with 9_7 and 14_6

2. *As from the darkening gloom a silver dove* (31)
   [December 1814 (publ. 1876)]
   P_{2a}: Petrarchan with cdcd cd

3. *To Lord Byron* (31)
[December 1814 (publ. 1848)]
P_{2a}: Petrarchan with <u>cdcd</u> cd

4. *O Chatterton! how very sad thy fate* (32)
[1815 (publ. 1848)]
P_{2a}: Petrarchan with <u>cdcd</u> cd

5. *Written on the Day That Mr. Leigh Hunt Left Prison (32)
[2 February 1815; *1817*, III)]
P_{2a}: Petrarchan with <u>cdcd</u> cd

6. *Woman! when I behold thee flippant, vain (40)
[1815–16; *1817*]
P_{2a}: Petrarchan with <u>cdcd</u> cd

7. *Light feet, dark violet eyes, and parted hair (40)
[1815–16; *1817*]
P_{2a}: Petrarchan with <u>cdcd</u> cd

8. *Ah! who can e'er forget so fair a being? (40–41)
[1815–16; *1817*]
P_{2a}: Petrarchan with <u>cdcd</u> cd

9. *O Solitude! if I must with thee dwell (41)
[?1815; pub *Ex.* 5 May 1816; *1817*, VII]
P_{3a}: Petrarchan with <u>cddc</u> dc

10. *Had I a man's fair form, then might my sighs (44)
[? 1815 or 1816; *1817*, II]
P_1: Petrarchan with <u>cde</u> cde

11. *To one who has been long in city pent (53–54)
[June 1816; *1817*, X]
P_{2a}: Petrarchan with <u>cdcd</u> cd

12. *Oh! how I love, on a fair summer's eve* (54)
[1816 (publ. 1848)]
P_1: Petrarchan with <u>cde</u> cde

13. *To a Friend Who Sent Me Some Roses (54–55)
    [29 June 1816; *1817*, V]
    P_{2a+}: Petrarchan with <u>cdcd</u> cd and 14_6

14. *Happy is England! I could be content (55)
    [?1816; *1817*, XVII]
    P_4: Petrarchan with c <u>dede</u> c

15. *To My Brother George (55–56)
    [August 1816; *1817*, I]
    H_P: Hybrid: P octave, S sestet (<u>cdcd</u> <u>ee</u>)

16. *How many bards gild the lapses of time (63–64)
    [?1816; *1817*, IV]
    P_{3a}: Petrarchan with <u>cddc</u> dc

17. *On First Looking into Chapman's Homer (64)
    [October 1816; *The Examiner*, 1 December 1816; *1817*, XI]
    P_{2a}: Petrarchan with <u>cdcd</u> cd

18. *Keen, fitful gusts are whisp'ring here and there (64–65)
    [October/November 1816; *1817*, IX]
    P_{2a}: Petrarchan with <u>cdcd</u> cd

19. *On Leaving Some Friends at an Early Hour (65)
    [October/November 1816; *1817*, XII]
    P_1: Petrarchan with <u>cde</u> <u>cde</u>

20. *To My Brothers (66)
    [18 November 1816; *1817*, VIII]
    P_{2a}: Petrarchan with <u>cdcd</u> cd

21. *Addressed to Haydon ["Highmindedness"] (66–67)
    [1816; *1817*, XIII]
    P_{2a}: Petrarchan with <u>cdcd</u> cd

22. *Addressed to the Same ["Great spirits"] (67)
    [20 November 1816; *1817*, XIV]
    P_{2a-}: Petrarchan with <u>cdcd</u> [c-]d [shortened 5th line]

23. *To G. A. W. (67–68) [Nymph of the downward smile] (67–68)
     [December 1816; *1817*, VI]
        P_{2a}: Petrarchan with <u>cdcd</u> cd

24. *To Kosciusko (68)
     [December 1816; *The Examiner*, 16 February 1817; *1817*, XVI]
        P_5: Petrarchan with cdedce (no quatrain or tercets)

25. *Written in Disgust of Vulgar Superstition* (88)
     [22 December 1816 (publ. 1876); Tom adds "Written in 15
        Minutes" to his draft]
        P_{2b}: Petrarchan with <u>cdcd</u> dc

26. *On the Grasshopper and Cricket (88–89)
     [30 December 1816; *1817*, XV]
        P_1: Petrarchan with <u>cde cde</u>

27. * –After dark vapours have oppressed our plains (89)
     [31 January 1817; *Ex.* 12 February 1817 (publ. 1848)]
        P_5: Petrarchan with cdefdf (no quatrain or tercets)

28. *To a Young Lady Who Sent Me a Laurel Crown* (89–90)
     [?1816/1817 (publ. 1848)]
        P_{2a}: Petrarchan with <u>cdcd</u> cd

29. *On Receiving a Laurel Crown from Leigh Hunt* (90)
     [end 1816 or early 1817 (publ. *Times* 1914)]
        P_{2a}: Petrarchan with <u>cdcd</u> cd

30. *To the Ladies Who Saw Me Crown'd* (90–91)
     [end 1816 or early 1817 (publ. *Times* 1914)]
        P_1: Petrarchan with <u>cde cde</u>

31. * –This pleasant tale is like a little copse (92)
     [February 1817; *The Examiner*, 16 March 1817; *Morning
        Chronicle, 17 March 1817 (publ. 1835)]*
        P_{3b}: Petrarchan with <u>cddc</u> ee

32. *To Leigh Hunt, Esq. (92–93)
   [February 1817; *1817*, Dedication]
      P$_{2a}$: Petrarchan with <u>cdcd</u> cd

SONNETS WRITTEN AFTER *POEMS 1817*

33. **On Seeing the Elgin Marbles (93)
   [March 1817; *The Champion*, 9 March 1817; *The Examiner*,
      9 March 1817; *Annals of the Fine Arts*, April 1818
      (publ. 1848)]
      P$_{2a}$: Petrarchan with <u>cdcd</u> cd

34. **To Haydon with a Sonnet Written on Seeing the Elgin Marbles
   (93)
   [March 1817; *Champion* and *Examiner* and *Annals* as above;
      (publ. 1848)]
      P$_{2a}$: Petrarchan with <u>cdcd</u> cd

35. On a Leander Which Miss Reynolds, My Kind Friend, Gave Me (94)
   [March 1817 (publ. *The Gem*, 1829)]
      P$_4$: Petrarchan with c <u>dede</u> c

36. On *The Story of Rimini* (95)
   [March 1817 (publ. 1848)]
      P$_{2a}$: Petrarchan with <u>cdcd</u> cd

37. **On the Sea (95)
   [17 April 1817 in L to J. H. Reynolds; *The Champion*,
      17 August 1817 (publ. 1848)]
      P$_4$: Petrarchan with c <u>dede</u> c

38. Before he went to live with owls and bats (98–99)
   [?1817 (publ. 1896)]
      P$_1$: Petrarchan with <u>cde</u> <u>cde</u>

ENDYMION (enjambed couplets)

39. To Mrs. Reynold's Cat (222)
   [16 January 1818 (publ. 1830)]
   P_{2a}: Petrarchan with cdcd cd

40. On Sitting Down to Read *King Lear* Once Again (225)
   [22 January 1818 (publ. 1838)]
   H_{1+}: Hybrid: P octave plus S sestet plus 14_6

41. When I have fears that I may cease to be (225–226)
   [end January 1818; lost letter to J. Reynolds of 31 January
      (publ. 1848)]
   S: Shakespearean

42. Time's sea hath been five years at its slow ebb (232)
   [4 February 1818 (publ. *Hood's Magazine,* 1844; 1848)]
   S: Shakespearean

43. To the Nile (233)
   [4 February 1818 (pub. 1838 and 1848)]
   P_{2a}: Petrarchan plus cdcd cd

44. Spenser, a jealous honorer of thine (233–234)
   [5 February 1818 (publ. 1848)]
   S: Shakespearean

45. Blue!—'Tis the life of heaven—the domain (234)
   [8 February 1818 (publ. 1848)]
   S: Shakespearean

46. O thou whose face hath felt the winter's wind (235)
   [19 February 1818 L to J. H. Reynolds (pub. 1848)]
   U: unrhymed, but sense units are two end-stopped quatrains,
      an end-stopped couplet, and a final quatrain, therefore
      tending toward Shakespearean form.

47. **Four seasons fill the measure of the year (238)
    [6–7 March; in 13 March 1818 L to Bailey; *Pocket-Book,* 1818
        (publ. 1829)]
    S: Shakespearean

48. To J. R. [James Rice] (244) ["O that a week"] (244)
    [?April 1818 (publ. 1848)]
    S: Shakespearean

ISABELLA (**ottava rima**)

49. To Homer (264)
    [1818 (publ. 1848)]
    S: Shakespearean

50. On Visiting the Tomb of Burns (266)
    [1 July 1818 in lost letter to Tom of that date, transcr.
        Jeffrey (publ. 1848)]
    P₄: Petrarchan with c <u>dede</u> c

51. **To Ailsa Rock (272)
    [10 July 1818; in 10–14 July 1818 L to Tom; *Pocket-Book,* 1819
        (publ. 1828)]
    P₂ₐ: Petrarchan with <u>cdcd</u> cd

52. This mortal body of a thousand days (272)
    [11 July 1818 (publ. 1848)]
    S: Shakespearean

53. Of late two dainties were before me plac'd (274–275)
    [18 July 1818; from 17–21 July 1818 L to Tom (publ. 1873)]
    H₁: Hybrid: Petrarchan octave with Shakespearean sestet

54. Read me a lesson, Muse, and speak it loud (279)
    [2 August 1818; in 3, 6 August 1818 L to Tom (publ. 1838)]
    S: Shakespearean

55. Nature withheld Cassandra in the skies (285–286): DOUZAIN
     [21 September 1818 (publ. 1848)]
          D: douzain, rhyming irregularly abab caca dede, therefore
          closer to Shakespearean model, although French original is
          Petrarchan.

THE EVE OF ST. AGNES (**Spenserian stanzas**)

56. Why did I laugh tonight? No voice will tell (323)
     [March 1819; in 14 February-3 May, 1819 L to George and
          Georgiana Keats (publ. 1848)]
          S: Shakespearean

57. **As Hermes once took to his feathers light (326)
     [April 1819; in 16 May L to George and Georgiana Keats;
          The Indicator 1820; *The London Magazine* 1821 (publ. 1837,
          1848)]
          S^+: Shakespearean with 14_6

58. Bright star, would I were stedfast as thou art (327–328)
     [1819 (publ. 1838)]
          S: Shakespearean

HYPERION (**blank verse**)

59. Sonnet to Sleep (363–364)
     [?end April 1819; in 14 February-3 May, 1819 L to George and
          Georgiana Keats (publ. 1838)]
          I: Irregularly rhymed with S octave: abab cdcd bc efef

60. On Fame (366–367) [Fame, like a wayward girl] (366–367)
     [30 April 1819; in 14 February-3 May, 1819 L to George and
          Georgiana Keats (publ. 1837, 1848)]
          S: Shakespearean

61. On Fame (367) [How fever'd is the man] (367)
     [30 April 1819; in 14 February-3 May, 1819 L to George and
          Georgiana Keats (publ. 1848]
          I: Irregularly rhymed with S octave: abab cdcd efe gg f

62. If by dull rhymes our English must be chain'd (368)
    [on or before 3 May 1819; in 14 February-3 May, 1819 L to
        George and Georgiana Keats (publ. 1836, 1848)]
      I: Irregularly rhymed: abc ab(d)c abc dede (tercets, quatrain)

OTHO THE GREAT **(blank verse)**

LAMIA **(heroic couplets)**

THE FALL OF HYPERION **(blank verse)**

63. The day is gone, and all its sweets are gone (491–492)
    [1819 (publ. 1838, 1848)]
      S: Shakespearean

64. I cry your mercy—pity—love!—aye, love (492)
    [1819 (publ. 1848)]
      S: Shakespearean

3

T. S. ELIOT

Inventing Prufrock

O lord, have patience
Pardon these derelictions—
I shall convince these romantic irritations
By my classical convictions.
        T. S. Eliot, manuscript leaf[1]

The debts of poets to their own earlier work are apt to be over-
looked. . . . Every man who writes poetry . . . will be dissatisfied
with his expressions and will want to employ the initial feeling, the
original image or rhythm, once more in order to satisfy himself.
        T. S. Eliot, "Poets' Borrowings"[2]

Do I know how I feel? Do I know what I think?
Let me take ink and paper, let me take pen and ink.
        (*March Hare*, 80)

C OMING OF AGE, for most people, means making decisions
about one's convictions, allegiances, and attachments. For po-
ets, coming of age requires as well finding one's own distinctive lan-
guage, one's idiolect, and it is this problem I especially address in
T. S. Eliot. Now that Christopher Ricks has edited and magnificently
annotated Eliot's early poems (1909–1917) in *Inventions of the March
Hare*, we are in a better position to understand how Eliot saw his
own apprentice writing, and how he trained himself so that he could,
in his twenties, write his first great poem, *The Love Song of J. Alfred
Prufrock*. In focusing on Eliot's early "Curtain Raisers"—a phrase I
borrow from the self-deprecating poet himself—I don't mean to
claim for these predecessors to *Prufrock* either greatness or literary
permanence. Yet they all show an intense desire to find a set of avail-
able discourses through which to present very intractable material.

That intractable material troubling the young Eliot would include
(in rough summary) a Puritanical suspicion of sex combined with
romantic sexual longing; a high sense of the historical tradition of

poetry together with a conviction that poetry must belong to its contemporary moment; an intense analytic intellectuality combined with a desire for drama (even melodrama); a pervasive attraction to religion without adult attachment to any church; and a New England propriety struggling with a withering irony. The intellectuality contended against the sexuality, the irony against the melodrama, the conventionality against the romanticism. Though Eliot, like any beginner, needed to find structures and genres suitable to his material, his first imaginative priority, given the musicality of his ear, was to find discourses—extended systems of language—to give voice to the qualities warring within him. Taking a cue from Browning, Eliot sometimes projected these aesthetic, sexual, and intellectual emotions onto dramatic characters. Yet the inner lyric self wanted its say too, and that directly personal voice alternates, in the young writer, with the voices externalized in dramatic personae. I want to consider here the discourses available to the young Eliot which he draws on, and perfects, in writing the 1911 *Love Song of J. Alfred Prufrock*.

Eliot returned again and again, in his prose, to the dilemma of idiom that he and other young American poets of his generation encountered as they came of age. There were simply no older poets on the English or American scene to adopt as models: "I do not think it is too sweeping to say," Eliot wrote retrospectively in 1946, "that there was no poet, in either country, who could have been of use to a beginner in 1908. . . . Browning was more of a hindrance than a help, for he had gone some way, but not far enough, in discovering a contemporary idiom. . . . The question was still: where do we go from Swinburne? and the answer appeared to be, nowhere."[3] "The only recourse," Eliot continued, "was to poetry of another age and to poetry of another language"; and, as we know, he turned to Dante for the first, to modern France for the second.

In Dante (revived in New England by Longfellow) Eliot found a discourse of theology both stricter and more intellectually complex than that purveyed by his Protestant upbringing; though this Dantean discourse sustained his long spiritual quest, he was unable to make prolonged poetic use of it until he wrote the *Quartets*.

Among the French poets, Baudelaire and Laforgue were the most important to him. The contribution of Baudelaire was less of idiom than of theme, as he showed the fastidious young Eliot "the poetic possibilities . . . of the more sordid aspects of the modern metropolis," "the possibility of fusion between the sordidly realistic and the phantasmagoric." But Laforgue bequeathed to Eliot the crucial gift of idiom—of actual modern linguistic sequences and tones through which words might be satisfyingly assembled. As Eliot recalled in 1950, "Of Jules Laforgue, for instance, I can say that he was the first to teach me how to speak, to teach me the poetic possibilities of my own idiom of speech." Both in temperament and in form of expression, Laforgue was "like an admired elder brother."[4]

It is sometimes forgotten that among the chief historical contexts for a young poet are the discourses to which he awakes when he becomes self-conscious about the use of language. First of all, every young writer finds himself historically situated in deep-rooted familial and educational discourses, which seem always already known. Even if a writer such as Dickinson chooses to remain solidly within those discourses familiar since childhood, she will necessarily use them blasphemously or at least peculiarly in order to transform them into an idiom of her own. Eliot doesn't feel able to dispense entirely with the manner of expression given him by his familial and educational culture; but he finds it especially inadequate—given its stoic reticence and linguistic formality—for the conveying of uneasy relations between the sexes and the voicing of inner torment. In addition to his inherited familial and school discourses, the young writer hears around him the sociolect of his own generation, and has to decide how much of it he wishes to take aboard, individualize, and make his own.

As Eliot experiments in language through the early poems, he tries out the discourses, familial and modern, native and foreign, available to him, modifying and extending these forms of speech to create a new poetry of sexual and psychological conflict. His experiments culminate in his first wholly successful poem—a strange lyric, pretending to be a dramatic monologue, called *The Love Song of J. Alfred*

Prufrock, to which this whole chapter tends. (I'll also be considering the uneasy fragment entitled *Prufrock's Pervigilium*, inserted, in the *March Hare* notebook, between lines 69 and 75 of *Prufrock*, but deleted by Eliot before publication.)[5]

The code of speech of Eliot's upper-class Protestant milieu was almost inhumanly restrained in what it allowed by way of permissible conversation between the sexes. Women especially were in general confined to a virginal modesty coupled with acceptably superficial "cultural" interests: "In the room the women come and go / Talking of Michelangelo." In some respects, Eliot's mother gave him a different model of female discourse: she was herself a poet, well-read and intellectually serious. Yet Eliot himself strikingly illustrates the conversational reticence that obtained between mother and son after Charlotte Eliot was shown—not by her son but by another person—his adolescent poems published in the school paper. "She remarked (we were walking along Beaumont Street in St. Louis) that she thought them better than anything in verse she had ever written. I knew what her verse meant to her. We did not discuss the matter further."[6] In spite of the importance to Eliot of the exchange—he recalls the very moment and place of its occurrence—there is perhaps no sentence more revealing of the family manner than Eliot's taciturn close: "We did not discuss the matter further."

Though in this instance there existed a silent mutual understanding between mother and son, Puritan verbal inhibition of this sort, when it appears in Eliot's poetry, usually betokens an inert non-mutuality. Although the motions of social intercourse are mimed, no contact of mind or soul takes place. Such conversations—anguishing for one who cares about authenticity in personal expression—can, torturingly, be continued over a long period, as in the 1910 *Portrait of a Lady* (Eliot's most ambitious poem preceding *Prufrock*, and, like *Prufrock*, a dramatic monologue). The inveigling and exploitative hostess, bidding farewell to her young acquaintance as he "betrays" her by going abroad, wonders "Why we have not developed into friends." The young man, for his part, feeling wholly hypocritical in the presence of her velleities and insinuations, all those "things to be said, or left unsaid," bitterly satirizes to himself his own participation in those brittle and sterile conversations wherein she sets the tone:

> And I . . . must borrow every changing shape
> For my expression—dance dance
> Dance like a dancing bear,
> Whistle like a parrot, chatter like an ape.
> (*MH*, 330)

Tellingly, no words spoken aloud by the young man appear in *Portrait of a Lady*, though we know that he has, in his conventional promenades with his patroness, verbally "admire[d] the monuments, discusse[d] the late events." In the *Portrait*, Eliot is unable to find an utterable public idiom for his male surrogate (who evokes his own speech only by the debasing self-descriptions "whistle" and "chatter"); consequently, he presents the young man only by his interior monologue. The words that Eliot presumably heard himself saying aloud, in false social situations of the sort underlying this poem, were so inauthentic that he could not bear to reproduce them in written form. In *Prufrock*, by contrast, he achieves a form of speech, however ironic, that his lyric surrogate, Prufrock, can speak aloud.

If conversations such as those described in *Portrait of a Lady* had occurred only occasionally in Eliot's social context, he would not have reacted to them so strongly. The absolute predictability of the script provided for young men and women of his class was to him a terrifying threat to genuineness of voice. The very first item in the notebook containing the *March Hare* poems has as its proposed title *Conversation Galante* (changed in the 1917 *Prufrock* volume to *Short Romance*). In this courting conversation, the prototypical young man is actually given a voice. We hear him trying to speak to a young woman earnestly (even if ironically at first) of landscape, music, and poetry; but the woman, restless because he is not playing the expected game of flirtation, dismisses his remarks with bored and irritated one-line replies. As the young man ventures, tentatively and truthfully, the observation that we seize on "music . . . / To body out our own vacuity," the young woman exclaims petulantly "Does this refer to me?" leaving the humiliated suitor to reply, "Oh no, it is I who am inane" (*MH*, 346).

The only envisaged purpose, in Eliot's society, of such *conversations galantes* was marriage. The young woman waits for the ritualized discourse to end in a proposal, and with each vacuous meeting the young man feels increasing pressure to declare himself. The moves are foreknown, and in the second poem of the notebook, Eliot discloses the speech-acts of upper-class courtship in all their monotony:

> Two, in a garden scene
> Go picking tissue paper roses;
> Hero and heroine, alone,
> The monotone
> Of promises and compliments
> And guesses and supposes.
> (*MH*, 11)

In an even more sexually dangerous move for the young man, the *conversation galante* can progress to the permitted physical conversation of young bodies in a waltz, as predictably recurrent as the feints of the garden:

> Always the August evenings come
> With preparation for the waltz . . .
> And the waltzes turn, return;
> The *Chocolate Soldier* assaults
> The tired Sphinx of the physical.
> What answer? We cannot discern.
> (*MH*, 26)

The repeatedly interrogated "tired Sphinx of the physical" doesn't reveal what one is to do with one's bodily desires in a society so conventional that every August waltz-evening resembles those of years before. The social rituals Eliot knew so well—those "verandah customs" of "White flannel ceremonial / With cakes and tea"—irritated him by their very pretense of intellectual seriousness, as guests hazarded "Guesses at eternal truths / Sounding the depths with a silver spoon" (*MH*, 28). This first sketch for *Prufrock* (a poem entitled *Goldfish*) shows us a speaker still bound by "verandah customs," unable to bow out of social expectations. Still worse, when this young man imagines himself refusing to conform, he fears that the role he will invent will be even more ridiculous than the one he refuses. (When Eliot's father changed his will, he must have seen his son's flight to England, poetry, and an unsuitable marriage in this light.) Equally unable to obey convention or to defy it, the young man fears, in *Suite Clownesque,* that he may become an indecisive and self-satisfied clownish figure, a "jellyfish impertinent," futilely aspiring to a relation with the absolute:

> Among the potted palms, the lawns,
> The cigarettes and serenades
>
> Here's the comedian again
> With broad dogmatic vest, and nose
> Nose that interrogates the stars.
> (*MH*, 32)

At least the Laforguian clown is not addressing "promises and compliments" to ladies, but instead is interrogating the stars—yet even that celestial conversation comes under Eliot's withering irony—"It's all philosophy and art." (The object of useless aspiration is later to be specified as "Michelangelo," the creator most saliently combining "philosophy and art.") New England's bankrupt social discourse for philosophical and aesthetic conversation seems to Eliot as limiting as its courtship-discourse.

One feels in all these early poems the desperate hunger of a young artist casting about for the "right" discourse for himself. Even the Laforguian sophistication so useful in *Portrait of a Lady* threatens to come to a dead end in the terminal irony underlying the self-deriding figure of the clown, that cousin to the drawing-room parrot and ape. The desired new poetic discourse doesn't yet exist, and can't be found in distaste and derision alone. Eliot must find the means to create it.

To avoid the empty verbal exchanges of meaningless courtship rituals, and the feared clownish image of himself as seen by others, Eliot turns his back on the erotic social scene and writes poems (such as *First Caprice in North Cambridge*) which record solitary evening wanderings through streets of mud and broken glass. In these verses, he simplifies his search for a viable idiom by remaining alone, and placing human voices or music in a distant or unthreatening position. Human sound is too far away to convey distinguishable meaning, as the wanderer hears only "broken flutes at garret windows" (*MH*, 16) or "a street-piano, garrulous and frail / . . . and the distant strains of children's voices" (*MH*, 13); or else human sound is naïve, small, and sexless, as in the voice of the innocent "little negro girl" who "repeats her little formulae of God" (*MH*, 23). Because the children's voices are not aimed at the speaker, they require of him no social interaction. This flight into solitude, accompanied solely by instrumental music, on the one hand, or childish noises or formulae, on the other, remains an evasion, rather than a solution, of the poet's central problem: how to embody in art those adult "human voices"—including his own—to which Eliot wakes in society and in which (as Prufrock) he drowns. Eliot—always an echo-chamber for all available discourses—finds inherited adult speech-patterns frustratingly unavailable for his poetic idiom precisely because they reiterate themselves so predictably in his mind, as the worn gramophone of memory rehearses its too well known aesthetic, social, philosophical, and romantic discourses.

Eliot was aesthetically interested not only in the exquisitely tuned meaningless speech-acts of social exchange—promises, compliments, guesses, supposes—but also in philosophical propositions, which were of supreme ethical consequence to him. He had to find some way to take seriously his own universalizing propositional discourse about things social, aesthetic, and ethical. Yet again and again, the early poems, after some tentative venturings into lyric seriousness, close by turning on themselves in self-mockery:

> Oh, these minor considerations! . . .
> (*First Caprice in North Cambridge, MH,* 13)

> But why are we so hard to please?
> (*Fourth Caprice in Montparnasse, MH,* 14)

> (What: again?)
> (*Second Caprice in North Cambridge, MH,* 15)

> These emotional experiences
> Do not hold good at all[.]
> (*Opera, MH,* 17)

> Inconsequent, intolerable.
> (*Goldfish I, MH,* 26)

> Philosophy through a paper straw!
> (*Goldfish II, MH,* 27)

These throwaway undoings of an anteriorly-voiced serious emotion can be summed up in the words of the oracle of the sibyl in *Goldfish* IV: "These problems seem importunate / But after all do not exist" (*MH,* 29).

Eliot couldn't go on pretending that his importunate problems—both of feeling and of expression—didn't exist. If mockery of upper-class conversational exchanges didn't suit, if burlesque via the personae of his Laforguian marionette-clowns didn't satisfy, he might turn to discourses, however vulgar, that were new—those being invented by his own generation. He could try to satirize modernity by experimenting with the catchy rhythm and arrantly theatrical self-presentation of the music hall, an idiom which had begun to enter his ear as seductively as verandah conversations or French irony:

> If you're walking up Broadway
> Under the light of the silvery moon,
> You may find me
> All the girls behind me
> Euphorion of the modern time
> Improved and up to date—sublime
> Quite at home in the universe
> Shaking cocktails on a hearse.
>   (*MH*, 35)

But for all the speaker's mocking efforts to adopt contemporary cocktail-party chatter and Tin-Pan-Alley rhythms—which are at least differently scripted from the Protestant mating ritual—he once again encounters sexual failure, because he cannot help reverting from Broadway to his own people, embalmed in their traditional summer wear. We see—as *Suite Clownesque* continues—the first adumbration of Prufrock and the mermaids, as the swimsuited flappers of the jazz age jeer at the beflanneled Brahmin bachelor:

> If you're walking on the beach
> You hear everyone remark
> Look at him!
> You will find me looking them over
> When the girls are ready for a swim
> Just out of reach
> First born child of the absolute
> Neat, complete,
> In the quintessential flannel suit.
>   (*Suite Clownesque III, MH*, 35)

The rituals of vaudeville and the music hall never ceased to appeal to Eliot, but—given their limitations as vehicles of extended lyric—they were to find their eventual and limited home (after a thrilling moment in *Sweeney Agonistes*) in *Old Possum's Book of Practical Cats*. Just as we've seen Eliot repudiate (in *Portrait of a Lady*) the mannered discourse of a *cavaliere servente* and (in *Conversation Galante*) the empty promises expected of a young suitor, so we'll see him forsake the dogmas and interrogations of the clown and the jazz idiom of the music-hall habitué. He can't, however, abandon irony and a sense of absurdity; they are constitutive of his sensibility.

We might pause for a moment to reflect on another aspect of Eliot's perplexity concerning a viable lyric discourse. We know that his interest in philosophical idiom was always intense; yet this preoccupation had not found a way to enter the early verse except as self-parody via the philosophical clown. Perhaps the young poet hadn't found a way of being philosophically serious in verse because the mode of discourse that he had discovered through philosophy was more negative than positive, more subtractive than contributory. In 1924, he wrote autobiographically about the capacity of philosophical investigation to erase both meaning and desire:

> If it ends, as it may well end, in zero, well, we have at least the satisfaction of having pursued something to the end, and of having ascertained that certain questions which occur to men to ask, are unanswerable or are meaningless. . . . You are led . . . to something which, according to your temperament, will be resignation or despair—the bewildered despair of wondering why you ever wanted anything, and what it was that you wanted, since this philosophy seems to give you everything that you ask and yet to render it not worth wanting.[7]

The corrosive acid of such a view prohibited, for Eliot, any positive use of the idiom of philosophical assertion until it could be backed for him by the theological certainty of faith.

When the young Eliot tries to speak lyrically, in a pure way, without the disguise of social manners or parody or clownishness or rag-time slang, what emerges is nineties bathos, as we see in some gothic, paranoid, and melodramatic lines of *Prufrock's Pervigilium* (the fragment added to, and then deleted from, *The Love Song of J. Alfred Prufrock*):

> I have gone at night through narrow streets,
>   Where evil houses leaning all together
> Pointed a ribald finger at me in the darkness
>   Whispering all together, chuckled at me in the darkness.
> [. . .]
>
> I fumbled to the window to experience the world
> And to hear my Madness singing, sitting on the kerbstone
> [A blind old drunken man who sings and mutters,
> With broken boot heels stained in many gutters]
> And as he sang the world began to fall apart . . .
>   (*MH*, 43)

This expressionist idiom of ribald fingers and stained boot heels would be impossible, as a long-term stylistic solution, for the exquisite Eliot. The self splits here, as the "I" separates from his own "Madness"—who is the only part of the self allowed singing voice. The song of Madness opposes the speaker's paranoid vision of the evil voices of the houses and the social world whispering and chuckling at him. As the "I"—who can only listen—permits autonomous lyric voice to his Madness, the world (like the self) falls apart.

As a refuge from dismissive parodic irony on the one hand, and explicit subjective bathos on the other, the young Eliot resorts, more successfully, to a middle discourse, which I will call the oblique. It differs from his previous poetic discourse in being serious but not propositional. It neither assents nor dissents. In lieu of declaratively explicit statements such as "the world began to fall apart," it offers forms of authentic feeling. In the oblique mode, feeling may express itself in any number of ways: it may utter a heartfelt exclamation, or hazard a suggestive image, or swerve from irony to inwardness. We find this oblique (non-assertive and non-propositional) discourse in the closing poem of *Suite Clownesque*, when after the ironic "last contortions of the dance . . . / the discovered masquerades / And the cigarettes and compliments," the speaker discovers that "through the painted colonnades / There falls a shadow dense, immense." The shadow turns out to be that of the clown; yet the *effect* of this intrusion, tonally, is to move the poem from brittle fiction to a haunting but non-gothic immediacy of feeling. (Eliot will take up this shadow-note of gravity in a later poem in which he replaces the parodic clown by lyric straw-stuffed hollow men.) In another oblique gesture, the 1911 poem *Entretien dans un parc* focuses on the moment of erotic commitment, in which a young man, seizing the hand of a young woman as they take a walk together, is allowed three lines of wholly unparodic reflection, descriptive, not propositional:

> It is not that life has taken a new decision—
> It has simply happened so to her and me.
>
> And yet this while we have not spoken a word.[8]

But almost immediately Eliot slips back into the old defensive and self-dismissing irony:

> It becomes at last a bit ridiculous
> And irritating. All the scene's absurd!
> (*MH*, 48)

Yet even as he dares to imagine a compelling truthfulness between lovers, he retreats to end the poem in his oblique manner—expressing neither assent nor repudiation—by means of an exclamatory allusion to Meredith's *Modern Love*:

> Some day, if God—
> But then, what opening out of dusty souls!
> (*MH*, 49)

Meredith's version in *Modern Love* reads, "Ah, what a dusty answer gets the soul / When hot for certainties in this our life!"

I've said earlier that for a writer, achieving emotional maturity is inseparable from achieving linguistic maturity. Eliot must find a path beyond merely ironizing the discourses given him by family, culture, and generation. Yet he knows that he remains in part a prisoner of those discourses that were around him as he began to write. His social class, especially, had imposed on him certain restrictions on aesthetic response, and nowhere is he more completely an aesthetic prisoner of his class than in the realm of sexuality. Had Eliot obeyed the mores of his society, he would have found himself married to one of those museum-going "ladies who are interested in Assyrian art" whom we encounter in the poem *Afternoon* (*MH*, 53). Though the phrase characterizing the ladies is resonant with satire, Eliot has begun to recognize that ethically it is not enough to offer sardonic portraits of the lives of Brahmins. He now finds, in these women's dim aspirations to something beyond their stifling lives, an analogy to his own search for a destination beyond, beneath, or above the self. As the museum-goers "fade beyond the Roman statuary . . . / Towards the unconscious, the ineffable, the absolute" (*MH*, 53), they are, in their way, repeating a yearning that Eliot knew well from his own experience. In his Clark Lectures, Eliot spoke of "the modern *recherche de l'absolu*, the disappointed romanticism, the vexation of resignation at finding the world other than one wanted it to be."[9] In spite of his rebellious, temporary, and ultimately mistaken escape to marriage with Vivienne Haigh-Wood, Eliot remained bound to a significant degree to the aesthetic and ethical standards of his class, embodied in his mother, whom he could not regard with mere contempt. This partial bondage to his historically given context made Eliot's search for an authentic aesthetic discourse the more distressing and arduous. His Protestant ethical seriousness had to find a way to share its own idiom with his satiric irony, his sexual revulsion, his love of philosophical language, his desire for a musical line, and his exacting sense of structural form.

Eliot later went so far, in a 1915 poem entitled *In the Department Store*, as to close a poem not with Laforguian irony, not even with an oblique image or allusive exclamation, but with a bleak and serious statement. As a frustrated and aging saleswoman dreams of past "heated nights in second story dance halls," the poet, contemplating her empty life, comments, "Man's life is powerless and brief and dark / It is not possible for me to make her happy" (*MH*, 56). This abjuring of irony, of bathos, of jazz-age slang, and even of poetic allusion (in favor of allusion, in this passage, to Bertrand Russell's prose volume of 1903, *A Free Man's Worship*) suggests that Eliot, even after discovering the possibilities of obliquity, was once again renewing his attempt to find an idiom in which he could be propositionally straightforward: "I would meet you upon this honestly" (as he was later to put it in *Gerontion*). He accomplishes this aim in *The Department Store* by speaking not of his own world falling apart, as in the *Pervigilium*, but by universalizing the tragedy: it is "man's life" that is dark.

Yet honesty for Eliot had to reach beyond impersonal philosophical reflection on "man's life" into something for which we have no name but intuition. He found ratification for his personal bafflement and anguish in the Christian theology of pain, and this led him to forms of religious discourse that we identify with his moments of stopped time, of inexplicable suffering, and of deliberate conversion. Surprisingly, this discourse of pain first appears in a secularized form in the notebook poem sardonically called *The Little Passion / From 'An Agony in the Garret.'* In it, the protagonist remarks that a line of city lights leads "To some inevitable cross / Whereon his soul is spread, and bleeds." This is the reading of the first draft: Eliot later generalized the line to the first-person plural, so that the lines of light lead "To some inevitable cross / Whereon our souls are pinned, and bleed." A torture resembling Prufrock's as he is "pinned and wriggling on the wall" is here given meaning by being identified, if only through the image of a cross, with the atoning suffering of Christ. And as Eliot forsakes for a moment his former tone of superiority to others, his personal suffering is given extension by being predicated collectively in the "we" that puts him within a human circle of companions.

In the 1914 poem *The Burnt Dancer* (*MH*, 62), written not long after *Prufrock*, Eliot will name his predicament as that of one "caught in the circle of desire" in "a world . . . / Too strange for good or evil." To enact his plight, he splits himself in two, just as he had in the *Pervigilium* when he separated his "I" from its artist-twin, "my Madness." In *The Burnt Dancer*, he splits his own "brain" from its inhabitant, the moth, who objectifies the expressive part of the speaker's own sensibility as an insect-artist-dancer, a third-person "patient acolyte of pain." The tortured dance of the moth in the flame is strictly bound in tight *abab* quatrains, mostly in tetrameter, anticipating those of the *Quartets*:

> Within the circle of my brain
> The twisted dance continues.
> The patient acolyte of pain,
> The strong beyond our human sinews,
> The singèd reveller of the fire,
> Caught on those horns that toss and toss,
> Losing the end of his desire
> Desires completion of his loss.
>   (*MH*, 62–63)

The "horns" on which the moth is (improbably) tossed seem to me those of the philosophical dilemmas raised earlier in the poem: the conflict between "more vital values" and the "golden values of the flame," between "agony" and "delight."[10]

The Burnt Dancer is less psychologically convincing, however, than the small, hideous undated prose poem *Introspection*, in which the mind is said to be sunk six feet deep in a cistern containing a self-tormenting imprisoned snake. (I reproduce Eliot's "unnatural" lineation: he wanted to have the prose resemble a cistern by confining it in a narrow "stanza.")

> The mind was six feet deep in a
> cistern and a brown snake with a tri-
> angular head having swallowed his
> tail was struggling like two fists
> interlocked. His head slipped along
> the brick wall, scraping at the
> cracks.
>
> (*MH*, 60)

Irony is useless for direct lyric representation of the poet's own pain, and superciliousness toward others is pointless once the poet recognizes himself as the cause of his own suffering. Eliot consequently turns here to a mythical symbol as an objective correlative of interior experience. The snake that swallows its own tail represents, with the obliquity of myth, a predicament—here, one of painful and fruitless introspection—that promises to be perpetual. Yet the *discourse* used of the archetypal ouroboros is anything but mythological. The snake-symbol is relentlessly naturalized as brown and triangular-headed, resembling "two fists interlocked," trapped in "a cistern." This raw realistic discourse, turning the airy "dance" of the brain-moth into the claustrophobic writhing of a brain-snake, makes introspection anything but transcendent. (The undated snake-image resembles that of Prufrock impaled and wriggling.)

A different impersonal symbol will be invoked by Eliot in the 1915 *Preludes* (IV, *Abenddämmerung, MH*, 335–336) as he imagines "The notion of some infinitely gentle / Infinitely suffering thing" which in an unexplained way acts as a companion and counterweight to his own desiccation. In such moments Eliot relies on symbolic discourse—the unadorned physicality of the moth and the snake on the one hand, and the transcendental concept of infinite suffering endured in infinite gentleness on the other—to voice those aspects of his own experience that are unamenable to irony. His poetic idiom must eventually stretch to encompass both—the most embodied and the most transcendent intuitions—giving to each aspect sympathetic understanding, symbolic representation, and lyric voice.

By the end of the *March Hare* notebook, Eliot has completed the fundamental arc of his search for a discourse adequate to his sensibility. He has mimicked, satirically, the inherited repressive discourses of his class, but has been unable to dismiss them utterly—admitting, by his recurrent recourse to such straitened exchanges, their importance in his aesthetic and ethical formation. He has fled gratefully at first to the foreign example of Laforgue, finding in irony a refuge from the inanities of both social and sexual upper-class conversation; he has nonetheless realized that ironic alienation cannot be a permanent discursive solution for a poet who also wants a lyric voice with which to speak directly and honestly on matters of the soul. He has judged the jazzy but semiotically empty discourse of the smart set as a language suitable only for "shaking cocktails on a hearse," usable as a decorative accent but not as a substantial matrix. He has found no stable poetic recourse, for the time being, in the Bradleian philosophical discourse that he could so expertly wield in prose, because philosophic questioning has brought him to a permanent skepticism in which not only truth, but all human desire, is canceled to "zero." (The *Quartets* will turn back to philosophical language and to Dante, because Eliot's religious conversion enables and supports—at least to his way of thinking—philosophical statement without skepticism, and theology within modernity.) Unable as yet to conclude for theological stability, but unsatisfied by the skeptical Bradleian philosophy of mind, the youthful Eliot makes literary allusion a communal guarantor of personal experience, turning to Browning for psychological projection, Meredith for the value of candor, Russell for support in philosophic despair, fable and myth for the introspective symbol, and a secularized New Testament (a cross with a small *c;* an infinitely suffering thing in lieu of a savior) for naturalized archetypes of psychological suffering.

Occasionally, in the poems of the *March Hare* notebook, the young Eliot dares projective introspection, looking at his worst sexual fantasies and writing them down, in a narrative discourse dependent on the decadent poets of the nineties. The 1914 *Love Song of St. Sebastian* ends in the grotesque:

You would love me because I should have strangled you
And because of my infamy;
And I should love you the more because I had mangled you
And because you were no longer beautiful
To anyone but me.
> (*MH*, 78)

(This combination of erotic desire and erotic victimization appears in *Prufrock* as well, but without the mangling and the strangling, without even the self-dramatizing "infamy.") Throughout the notebook, Eliot searches out language for all the twists and turns of his struggle with both desire and poetry, asking implicitly and explicitly the fundamental questions that he formulated in an undated piece of ironic doggerel:

Do I know how I feel? Do I know what I think?
Let me take ink and paper, let me take pen and ink.
> (*MH*, 80)

We come to the end of the *March Hare* notebook and find Eliot still preoccupied with the problem of how to incorporate into poetry the overheard discourse of others, those "little voices of the throats of men / That come between the singer and the song" (*MH*, 75). In the fascinating, if over-intellectualized, 1914 poem that opens with this fear of the social world as an impediment to lyric, the young Eliot comes closest to a full analysis of the dilemma of the modern poet:

Appearances appearances he said,
I have searched the world through dialectic ways;
I have questioned restless nights and torpid days,
And followed every by-way where it lead [*sic*];
And always find the same unvaried
Intolerable interminable maze. . . .
Appearances, appearances, he said,

And nowise real; unreal, and yet true;
Untrue, yet real;—of what are you afraid? . . .
. . . If you find no truth among the living
You will not find much truth among the dead.
No other time but now, no other place than here, he said.
    (*MH*, 75)

Eliot's courage lay first in evaluating the "dialectic ways" of the discourses he found available to him, and then in deciding finally for modernity of image and diction and voice while allowing these to be "thickened" by the implicit historicity and communal worth of literary allusions. For Eliot as a young lyric poet, there could be, in terms of theme and manner, no other time but now, no other place than here. In transcribing into his own first poetry the tormenting "human voices" that never left him alone, that drowned him when he woke to them, he finally invented, both with irony and without, a contemporary style amalgamating many discourses, both given and sought-for, into a personal idiom. This hard-won and original idiolect becomes fully visible for the first time in *Prufrock*.

The Love Song of J. Alfred Prufrock

S'io credesse che mia risposta fosse
A persona che mai tornasse al mondo,
Questa fiamma staria senza più scosse.
Ma perciocche giammai di questo fondo
Non tornò vivo alcun, s'i'odo il vero,
Senza tema d'infamia ti rispondo.[11]

Let us go then, you and I,
When the evening is spread out against the sky
Like a patient etherised upon a table;
Let us go, through certain half-deserted streets,
The muttering retreats
Of restless nights in one-night cheap hotels
And sawdust restaurants with oyster-shells:

Streets that follow like a tedious argument
Of insidious intent
To lead you to an overwhelming question . . .
Oh, do not ask, "What is it?"
Let us go and make our visit.

In the room the women come and go
Talking of Michelangelo.

The yellow fog that rubs its back upon the window-panes,
The yellow smoke that rubs its muzzle on the window-panes
Licked its tongue into the corners of the evening,
Lingered upon the pools that stand in drains,
Let fall upon its back the soot that falls from chimneys,
Slipped by the terrace, made a sudden leap,
And seeing that it was a soft October night,
Curled once about the house, and fell asleep.

And indeed there will be time
For the yellow smoke that slides along the street,
Rubbing its back upon the window-panes;
There will be time, there will be time
To prepare a face to meet the faces that you meet;
There will be time to murder and create,
And time for all the works and days of hands
That lift and drop a question on your plate;
Time for you and time for me,
And time yet for a hundred indecisions,
And for a hundred visions and revisions,
Before the taking of a toast and tea.

In the room the women come and go
Talking of Michelangelo.

And indeed there will be time
To wonder, "Do I dare?" and, "Do I dare?"

Time to turn back and descend the stair,
With a bald spot in the middle of my hair—
[They will say: "How his hair is growing thin!"]
My morning coat, my collar mounting firmly to the chin,
My necktie rich and modest, but asserted by a simple pin—
[They will say: "But how his arms and legs are thin!"]
Do I dare
Disturb the universe?
In a minute there is time
For decisions and revisions which a minute will reverse.

    For I have known them all already, known them all;
Have known the evenings, mornings, afternoons,
I have measured out my life with coffee spoons;
I know the voices dying with a dying fall
Beneath the music from a farther room.
    So how should I presume?

    And I have known the eyes already, known them all—
The eyes that fix you in a formulated phrase,
And when I am formulated, sprawling on a pin,
When I am pinned and wriggling on the wall,
Then how should I begin
To spit out all the butt-ends of my days and ways?
    And how should I presume?

    And I have known the arms already, known them all—
Arms that are braceleted and white and bare
[But in the lamplight, downed with light brown hair!]
Is it perfume from a dress
That makes me so digress?
Arms that lie along a table, or wrap about a shawl.
    And should I then presume?
    And how should I begin?

          . . . . .
Shall I say, I have gone at dusk through narrow streets

And watched the smoke that rises from the pipes
Of lonely men in shirt-sleeves, leaning out of windows? . . .

    I should have been a pair of ragged claws
Scuttling across the floors of silent seas.

     . . . . .

And the afternoon, the evening, sleeps so peacefully!
Smoothed by long fingers,
Asleep . . . tired . . . or it malingers,
Stretched on the floor, here beside you and me.
Should I, after tea and cakes and ices,
Have the strength to force the moment to its crisis?
But though I have wept and fasted, wept and prayed,
Though I have seen my head [grown slightly bald] brought
     in upon a platter,
I am no prophet—and here's no great matter;
I have seen the moment of my greatness flicker,
And I have seen the eternal Footman hold my coat, and
     snicker,
And in short, I was afraid.

    And would it have been worth it, after all,
After the cups, the marmalade, the tea,
Among the porcelain, among some talk of you and me,
Would it have been worth while,
To have bitten off the matter with a smile,
To have squeezed the universe into a ball
To roll it toward some overwhelming question,
To say: "I am Lazarus, come from the dead,
Come back to tell you all, I shall tell you all"—
If one, settling a pillow by her head,
    Should say: "That is not what I meant at all,
    That is not it, at all."

    And would it have been worth it, after all,
Would it have been worth while,

After the sunsets and the dooryards and the sprinkled streets,
After the novels, after the teacups, after the skirts that trail
    along the floor—
And this, and so much more?—
It is impossible to say just what I mean!
But as if a magic lantern threw the nerves in patterns on
    a screen:
Would it have been worth while
If one, settling a pillow or throwing off a shawl,
And turning toward the window, should say:
    "That is not it at all,
    That is not what I meant, at all."
     . . . . .

No! I am not Prince Hamlet, nor was meant to be;
Am an attendant lord, one that will do
To swell a progress, start a scene or two,
Advise the prince; no doubt, an easy tool,
Deferential, glad to be of use,
Politic, cautious, and meticulous;
Full of high sentence, but a bit obtuse;
At times, indeed, almost ridiculous—
Almost, at times, the Fool.

    I grow old . . . I grow old . . .
I shall wear the bottoms of my trousers rolled.

    Shall I part my hair behind? Do I dare to eat a peach?
I shall wear white flannel trousers, and walk upon the beach.
I have heard the mermaids singing, each to each.

    I do not think that they will sing to me.

    I have seen them riding seaward on the waves
Combing the white hair of the waves blown back
When the wind blows the water white and black.

We have lingered in the chambers of the sea
By sea-girls wreathed with seaweed red and brown
Till human voices wake us, and we drown.[12]

When, after reading the early verse, we return to Eliot's first "per-fect" poem, the long-familiar *Love Song of J. Alfred Prufrock* (sig-nificantly, it bore as its original title *Prufrock among the Women* [*MH*, 39]), we see it with new eyes, as a cento of almost all the dis-courses that Eliot had previously attempted. Yes, it takes its form from Browning's dramatic monologues, but the required listener of the Browning genre has here been radically diminished from his usual socially specified self (a wife, some "nephews," an envoy). Prufrock's companion has dwindled to the Cheshire invisibility of ear alone, as the speaker, aridly, truthfully, and lyrically, voices the Eliotic *incipit*—"Let us go then, you and I." The "you" is the Madness of the *Pervigilium*, the mind-moth of *The Burnt Dancer*, the mind-serpent of *Introspection*—now not alienated to a curbstone, a flame, or a cistern, but integrated as an inevitable, even necessary compan-ion. In *Prufrock*, motifs and voices of the early poems reappear—de-sire, fearful as it enters the social world of "love" and marriage pro-posals; guilty self-laceration; romantic aspiration; Laforguian irony; Baudelairean urban surroundings; philosophic doubt; literary allu-sion; lyric pain. But the balance among these motifs has reached an equilibrium not visible in the more derisory or gothic inventions of less successful poems. Eliot has not mastered any new techniques be-fore writing *Prufrock;* rather, he has learned to integrate, in a coher-ent style, the techniques he already knows, without having them ex-tinguish each other, without himself compulsively resorting, as he once had, to mocking or melodramatic endings that dismiss their precedent speculations. He dares to preface the poem with a serious epigraph from Dante's underworld. He has begun to see the poten-tial aesthetic value of his hatreds and his sufferings: not only will there be time to murder, there will be time to create. He dares to sug-gest—even if ironically—that his question might disturb the universe (a possibility that his early self-mocking discourses could not have allowed themselves to entertain). He fully enunciates (instead of merely mimicking or parodying) the fatigued repetitiveness of his doubt and his desire ("I have known them all already, known them all") while going forth yet again to the social world, his theater (now fully acknowledged) of lyric action. He is willing to include the rawest physicality of discourse: Prufrock's "wriggling" on a pin had been earlier phrased, equally unflinchingly, as "sprawling" and "squirming" (*MH*, 42).

Instead of representing himself by means of a single image—whether as a clown or a Pierrot or a murderer (or even as a young man on a verandah or in a parlor)—Eliot speculatively becomes (not without irony, but not without seriousness, either) John the Baptist, Hamlet, Lazarus, and a lover of mermaids. Most of all, he has discovered what his poetry—with its insidious rhythms, its hesitations, its etherized evening, its sleeping fog, its effortful confrontation of the moment's "crisis," its satiric sallies—is meant to do. It is to construct the effect "as if a magic lantern threw the nerves in patterns on a screen": that is, to function as an EEG, an image-coded graph of the twitches of the nerves as they respond to life's disorders, above all to the obsessive question of sexual desire. The exacerbated nerves vibrate sometimes towards anesthesia, sometimes towards energy; now towards disgust, now towards ennui; now towards cosmic fear, now towards social agony; now towards romantic longing, now towards a suicidal siren-song. In one superb effort of poetic concentration and polyphonic effect, the gamut of responses and discourses discovered through earlier poems is fluently explored, as a hypnotically alluring voice, sure of its own circuits of stylistic movement, invites us—"Let us go then, you and I."

Although I've mentioned the feelings, and the discourses, gathered up in *Prufrock,* I need to say a few words to show how the formal unity of the poem is attained, why the verse does not fracture along inner fault-lines of incompatible discourses. We have seen the damage done in *Prufrock's Pervigilium* when Eliot reifies and personifies and characterizes his Madness (blind, drunken, with stained boot heels, sitting on a curb). Eliot endangers that fragment, too, by the stutter of self-repeating end-words with feminine endings: *windows, blindness, corners, entries, flickered, papers, together, corner, together, darkness, darkness, fever, darkness, kerbstone, mutters, gutters*—16 such endings in 31 lines. The febrile effect of such end-words is, by contrast, carefully husbanded in the final *Prufrock*, where we find only *table, evening, chimneys, indecisions,* and *revisions;* and then nothing until *windows, fingers,* and *malingers.* Later, in a self-mocking cluster, there are *ices* and *crisis, platter* and *matter, flicker* and *snicker.* The last of such end-words is (fittingly) *question.* After the line in which it appears, where Prufrock imagines rolling the universe "toward some overwhelming question," there are no more lines with feminine end-words: the poem proceeds with solid accents on each end-line monosyllable, accompanied by such emphatic close-placed rhymes as *peach, beach,* and *each*):[13]

> I grow old . . . I grow old . . .
> I shall wear the bottoms of my trousers rolled.
>
>   Shall I part my hair behind? Do I dare to eat a peach?
> I shall wear white flannel trousers, and walk upon the beach.
> I have heard the mermaids singing, each to each.

Prufrock's Pervigilium suffers damage as well because it situates its speaker among Disneyfied gothic surroundings in which houses point ribald fingers and chuckle, the midnight writhes in fever, and the darkness, octopus-like, stretches out tentacles. *Prufrock* does not abandon the gothic altogether, but it domesticates it into the cat-like fog. When it does become high-pitched in its metaphors—as Prufrock is "pinned and wriggling on the wall," his mouth choked with "the butt-ends of [his] days and ways"—it keeps the moments of such outright agony far apart and relatively few. And instead of situating the protagonist in the dubious streets of the *Pervigilium,* where "Women, spilling out of corsets, stood in entries," it situates him in the social world normally inhabited by Eliot: the world of superficially cultivated women, drawing-rooms, and tea.

As we scan the first half of *Prufrock* for the discourses it brings to bear, we see, in sequence, these discourses (which I number for ease of subsequent reference):

1. the urban solitary (the sky, the restless nights, the restaurants, the streets);
2. the gothic descriptive (newly domesticated in fog);
3. the musing propositional ("there will be time . . . for visions and revisions");
4. the upper-class social ("toast and tea . . . talking of Michelangelo");
5. the personally ironic ("With a bald spot in the middle of my hair");
6. the philosophically interrogative ("Do I dare / Disturb the universe?");
7. the ennuyé ("I have known them all already, known them all");
8. the socially terrified ("When I am pinned and wriggling on the wall");
9. the erotic of attraction ("Arms that are braceleted and white and bare");
10. the erotic of revulsion ("But in the lamplight, downed with light brown hair!").

Halfway through the poem there appears Prufrock's first inserted lyric, with its three stanzas and its refrain in "How should I presume." After that lyric ceases, the poem becomes a formal reprise, recapitulating itself, as discourse 1 comes back in the "lonely men in shirt-sleeves, leaning out of windows," 2 in the ragged claws and the tired evening, 4 in the tea and cakes and ices, 5 in the bald head on the platter, 6 in squeezing the universe into a ball, 7 in "Would it have been worth it, after all," 8 in "the nerves in patterns on a screen," 9 in "the skirts that trail along the floor," and so on. During this recapitulation, Prufrock has sung his second lyric, two stanzas linked by their common beginning ("And would it have been worth it, after all") and end ("at all"). The two internal lyrics distinguish *Prufrock* from the Victorian dramatic monologues from which it derives, and assert the affiliation of its dramatic protagonist with its lyric author, who calls his dramatic monologue a "Love Song."

The penultimate part of the poem judges the self with mordant social ennui ("Almost, at times, the Fool"); but the last part sets mocking personal irony ("Do I dare to eat a peach?") against a stubborn romanticism derived from "the chambers of the sea" and the song of the mermaids. The reduplicative semiosis of the close is something new in Eliot:

```
have heard         the mermaids              singing      each to each
                   they will                 sing
have seen          them                      riding       sea-ward
                             on the waves
the         white hair      of the waves            blown            back
                                                    blows
            white                                                    black
have lingered                the chambers of the         sea
                                                          sea-girls
                                                          seaweed
```

This is the discourse of art aspiring to the condition of music, as the overlapping words are reinforced by intense alliteration and assonance. Such a discourse loses its affiliation with any functional social purpose. Its Paterian harmonics, self-referential and self-dissolving, make *Prufrock* end in obliquity—in a vision of mermaids who can neither be possessed nor forgotten.

Prufrock introduces himself with an impulsive anapestic step forward—"Let us *go*"—which immediately lapses into ordinary iambs: "Let us go, then, you and I." This anapestic impulse becomes Prufrock's rhythmic signature—the symbol of his willingness to make his social "visit." The impulse is most frequent at the beginning of the poem:

> Let us *go* then, you and I,
> When the *eve*ning is spread out against the sky
> Like a *pa*tient etherised upon a table;
> Let us *go*, through certain half-deserted streets . . .
> Let us *go* and make our visit.

Prufrock's *incipit* is rhythmically mocked by the dismissive woman: "That is *not* what I meant, at all." And by the end of the poem, the courageous little anapestic skip seems to have been trivialized: "Shall I *part* my hair behind? Do I *dare* to eat a peach?" With a renewal of imaginative courage, Prufrock, though a failure with "real" women, regains his skip as he claims a better acquaintance: "I have *heard* the mermaids singing, each to each." This resurgence of romance is followed by a line of sedulously depressed iambs: "I do not think that they will sing to me." Courageous once more, Prufrock insists: "I have *seen* them," and the landscape echoes his skip: "When the *wind* blows the water white and black." Prufrock's last anapest is, surprisingly, voiced in a collective "we" (not the "you and I" or "you and me" of the rest of the poem); it is the same "we" that we have seen him adopt when a religious or philosophical vision puts him in the suffering company of his fellow human beings: "We have *ling*ered in the chambers of the sea." By this "we" he means, of course, his social self and his artist-self ("Madness"), now companions in better-integrated experience; but he also means other human beings like himself. Although the last two lines let us drown to the music of iambs, the penultimate one is luxurious in reduplicative sound: "By sea-girls wreathed with seaweed red and brown."

Such small matters as anapests and assonance undergird the imaginative effort and the long lines of *The Love Song of J. Alfred Prufrock*. The poem aligns many internal discourses (all of them expressive of some aspect of Eliot's feelings) into one "social" narrative, and encloses within that linear narrative of the disappointing "visit" the more visibly patterned two "lyrics" of ennui. The lyrics are there to show "Madness singing"—and in fact it was after the first "ennui lyric" ("For I have known them all already, known them all") that Eliot left the four-page space in the original *Prufrock* into which he inserted the relatively regular four stanzas of *Prufrock's Pervigilium,* making a second densely-patterned "lyric" follow the first. In the canonical *Prufrock,* Eliot does not split the inner "songs" off from the narrative and ascribe them to his "Madness," an alienated and personified utterer; rather, he has decided to have the same voice uttering both the narrative and its internal lyrics. But in making the lyrics formally visible by means of their stanzaic grouping, Eliot is asserting that even though he has determined on the theater of the social as his lyric venue, he will not thereby be deprived of the intensity of personal song. (He will keep to this resolution, in altered ways, in the more patterned and song-like portions of the *Quartets.*)

The force driving *Prufrock* is Eliot's youthful desire to fuse, in his poetry, his alienated erotic self, his transfixed social self, his intellectual philosophic self, and his introspective artistic self, which we have seen separated out into various incompatible discourses in his early experiments in language. As the social self wanders with the artistic self through the evening streets and the drawing rooms of *Prufrock,* Eliot at last finds a single rich discourse which can absorb, pattern, and express them all. This discourse—Eliot's newly achieved personal style—is the foundation for *The Waste Land,* where he will complicate it by taking it out of the drawing-room and placing it in larger geographical, historical, and literary contexts. But that is another story.

4

SYLVIA PLATH

Reconstructing the Colossus

F EW YOUNG POETS have worked as hard as Sylvia Plath (1932–1963). Her intense and sustained practice of verse in her twenties can be seen in the fifty poems that Ted Hughes included in the *Collected Poems* under the title "Juvenilia"[1] (and these represent less than a quarter of the 221 pieces she wrote before she was twenty-five).[2] At twenty-seven, she wrote the poem that I propose as her first "perfect" one—*The Colossus*, which gave her initial volume (1960) its title. Though Plath would go on to do more powerful and more exquisite work, *The Colossus*—an elegy for the poet's father—is still the earliest poem that most anthologists of Plath include. Otto Plath, although a scientist himself, incomprehensibly self-diagnosed his diabetes as lung cancer, and refused medical treatment for four years. Eventually, after his leg was amputated because of diabetic gangrene, he died at 55 in November 1940 (shortly after his daughter's eighth birthday) of an embolism of the lung.[3] It is possible that he suffered during his illness from the profound depression that his daughter later experienced, but at eight she could not have known this: she felt (perhaps imitating her mother's feelings) that he had willfully abandoned her by a quasi-suicide. By her own account, Plath first attempted suicide at ten; even if the story is not true, it symbolizes her feelings after losing her father.[4]

Although the poet may have given her father's death too great an explanatory role in her own subsequent suffering—which we now ascribe in part to bipolar illness—it remains true that the bewildering death of Otto Plath perplexed his daughter's cognitive powers and dominated her imaginative ones for some time: its effect resonates throughout her adult verse, and is already present in nineteen poems preceding *Electra on Azalea Path* (see the appendix at the end of this chapter). The first mature poems treating her father's death are two elegies: *Electra*, the earlier of the two, not included in the *Colossus* volume,[5] and *The Colossus*, a much stronger poem, written seven months later. I want to compare these two poems (to the end of showing the brilliant work Plath was able to do in the second by repudiating the style of the first), and then I'll go on to a later poem,

Parliament Hill Fields, an elegy for an unborn child. This represents Plath's later reconceiving of the genre of elegy, bringing it out of the melodramatic mode of *Electra* and the static mode of *The Colossus*. It's a new sort of Plath poem, looking promisingly, if still awkwardly, for a social canvas wider than that of the claustrophobic elegies for the father. In allowing myself the liberty of a flash-forward, I want to show that although I believe *The Colossus* to be Plath's first "perfect" poem, I do not think it represents her best conception of what a poem should be. I will close with a still later elegy, *Edge*.

Electra on Azalea Path can give us a notion of the style Plath was working in during early 1959. And the journal notes that Plath kept on *Electra* (*CP*, 289) implicitly prophesy her later aims in writing *The Colossus*. (As Ted Hughes remarks in his Introduction to the *Collected Poems*, "Her evolution as a poet went rapidly through successive moults of style, as she realized her true matter and voice. . . . At each move we made, she seemed to shed a style" [*CP*, 16]). On March 9, 1959, a little more than eighteen years after Otto Plath's death, Plath went to the Winthrop, Massachusetts, graveyard where her father was buried, and, next to Azalea Path, found his tombstone:

> Went to my father's grave, a very depressing sight. . . . Headstones together, as if the dead were sleeping head to head in a poorhouse. . . . I found the flat stone: *Otto E. Plath: 1885–1940.* Right beside the path, where it would be walked over. Felt cheated. My temptation to dig him up. To prove he existed and really was dead. How far gone would he be? No trees, no peace, his headstone jammed up against the body on the other side. Left shortly.

On March 20, eleven days later, she wrote: "Finished . . . 'Electra on Azalea Path.' They [her current poems] are never perfect but I think have goodnesses." Yet a month later, on April 23, she repudiates the poem, saying, "Must do justice to my father's grave. Have rejected the Electra poem from my book. Too forced and rhetorical" (*CP*, 289). We are, then, to think of *The Colossus*, Plath's next poem on the same subject, as less "forced and rhetorical" in style than *Electra*; but to understand what these words meant to Plath, we need to look at the *Electra* of March 20 with Plath's own critical eyes of April 23. I think that by "forced and rhetorical" Plath chiefly meant "Lowellesque"; by October of 1959, when she was writing *The Colossus,* she had succeeded in shaking off Lowell's mannerisms.

Let me briefly describe the substance of *Electra on Azalea Path.* A daughter addresses her father (dead now for twenty years), announcing to him that after he died, she deliberately regressed into a colorless hibernation, a return to the womb, a repressive state of denial in which, on her controlled mental stage populated by "stony actors," "nobody died or withered." Now, acknowledging her father's death and beginning to allow the presence of grief, she has sought out his grave, deploring the stinted and artificially-decked space of the graveyard where he is buried. As she becomes aware of her "Electra-complex" (as Plath later described it on the BBC with respect to a different poem, *Daddy* [*CP,* 293]), the daughter suddenly leaves realistic description behind and, speaking as the Elektra of the *Oresteia,* addresses—in three italicized lines—her father Agamemnon, recalling his murder and his wife Clytemnestra's revenge for his sacrifice of their daughter Iphigenia. (Plath strips the quotation of any proper names: "my sister" and "my mother" are the reference-points of the passage spoken by Elektra.) The contemporary speaker of the poem—embarrassed by the disproportion between the *Oresteia* and her own domestic grief—explains her sudden plunge into ancient Greece in a self-deprecating tone: "I borrow the stilts of an old tragedy." Returning to realism (after noting two bad omens that had attended her own birth), she relates her father's death from gangrene and the blow it caused to her nascent emotional life: "I brought my love to bear, and then you died. . . . / I am the ghost of an infamous suicide." The poem closes with inexplicable guilt, as the daughter asks her father's pardon for causing his death as well as her own (posthumously-reported) envisaged suicide: "It was my love that did us both to death."

Electra is composed in five rhyming pentameter stanzas, alternately ten lines and eight lines long:

Electra on Azalea Path

The day you died I went into the dirt,
Into the lightless hibernaculum
Where bees, striped black and gold, sleep out the blizzard
Like hieratic stones, and the ground is hard.
It was good for twenty years, that wintering—
As if you had never existed, as if I came
God-fathered into the world from my mother's belly:
Her wide bed wore the stain of divinity.
I had nothing to do with guilt or anything
When I wormed back under my mother's heart.

Small as a doll in my dress of innocence
I lay dreaming your epic, image by image.
Nobody died or withered on that stage.
Everything took place in a durable whiteness.
The day I woke, I woke on Churchyard Hill.
I found your name, I found your bones and all
Enlisted in a cramped necropolis,
Your speckled stone askew by an iron fence.

In this charity ward, this poorhouse, where the dead
Crowd foot to foot, head to head, no flower
Breaks the soil. This is Azalea Path.
A field of burdock opens to the south.
Six feet of yellow gravel cover you.
The artificial red sage does not stir
In the basket of plastic evergreens they put
At the headstone next to yours, nor does it rot,
Although the rains dissolve a bloody dye:
The ersatz petals drip, and they drip red.

Another kind of redness bothers me:
The day your slack sail drank my sister's breath

The flat sea purpled like that evil cloth
My mother unrolled at your last homecoming.
I borrow the stilts of an old tragedy.
The truth is, one late October, at my birth-cry
A scorpion stung its head, an ill-starred thing;
My mother dreamed you face down in the sea.

The stony actors poise and pause for breath.
I brought my love to bear, and then you died.
It was the gangrene ate you to the bone
My mother said; you died like any man.
How shall I age into that state of mind?
I am the ghost of an infamous suicide,
My own blue razor rusting in my throat.
O pardon the one who knocks for pardon at
Your gate, father—your hound-bitch, daughter, friend.
It was my love that did us both to death.
            (*CP*, 116)

Embodying one of Plath's ingeniously original stanzaic structures,[6] *Electra* is nonetheless full of unassimilated thematic and stylistic echoes of other poets—Yeats, Frost, Owen, and above all Plath's teacher, Robert Lowell. Plath borrows conspicuously from Lowell's elegy called *At the Indian Killer's Grave*, as we can see from her adoption of Lowell's characteristic syntactic form: an enjambed front-loaded sentence immediately brought up short by a subsequent curt sentence:

In this charity ward, this poorhouse, where the dead
Crowd foot to foot, head to head, no flower
Breaks the soil. This is Azalea Path.

Plath also echoes Lowell's insistent rhetorical practice of repetition of words and syntactic parallels. Focusing with Lowellesque intensity on the basket of artificial flowers at a nearby grave, she describes the red sage among them with the chiasmus *red . . . drip . . . drip red,* reinforced alliteratively by *rot* and *rains::*

> The artificial red sage does not stir
> . . . nor does it rot,
> Although the rains dissolve a bloody dye:
> The ersatz petals drip, and they drip red.

Plath mimics the suicidal drive in Lowell as well, borrowing his image of the razor from *Waking in the Blue,* but (since she is at the moment speaking posthumously) altering it to a razor rusting after she has used it to kill herself:

> I am the ghost of an infamous suicide,
> My own blue razor rusting in my throat.

Imitating Yeats as another source of "the rhetorical," Plath declares: "I borrow the stilts of an old tragedy." (Yeats represented his own lofty rhetoric as "stilts" in *High Talk,* arguing that "Processions that lack high stilts have nothing that catches the eye.")[7] And Yeats's habit of assuming a mythical figure such as Cuchulain as a lyric persona may lie behind Plath's adoption of the figure of Electra, just as Yeats's bestowing of epic roles on characters in his life (Maud Gonne as Helen of Troy) may have influenced Plath's raising of her father to epic dimensions: "I lay dreaming your epic, image by image." Frost, too, turns up in *Electra:* the gravelly tone of his New Hampshire narratives can be heard behind certain of Plath's lines: "It was the gangrene ate you to the bone / My mother said; you died like any man." And the slant rhymes and off-rhymes that Plath uses are property lifted from Yeats and Owen ("stage" and "image"; "bone" and "man"; "throat" and "at").[8]

What then, we might ask—other than its ingenious if unconvincing alternating stanza-forms—is *not* derivative in *Electra on Azalea Path?* What can we ascribe to the imaginative invention of Plath herself? For the most part, her originality lies in the summoning of themes and images that will become part of her permanent repertoire. These include:

Symbiosis with the father ("The day you died I went into the dirt . . . / It was my love that did us both to death");

Trauma deliberately repressed ("It was good for twenty years, that wintering— / As if you had never existed . . . / Everything took place in a durable whiteness");

Bees and stones ("bees, striped black and gold, sleep out the blizzard / Like hieratic stones");

The daughter's divine origin ("I came / God-fathered into the world");

The self as inanimate ("Small as a doll in my dress of innocence");

The repetition in herself of her father's "suicide" ("How shall I age into that state of mind?").

The most noticeable uneasiness in *Electra on Azalea Plath* is the coexistence of the quasi-photographic replication of the graveyard (which Plath altered slightly from her prose notes) and the Greek epic machinery of the narrative. The poem registers strongly Plath's pain at the sheer *crowding* of the dead in the cemetery; she feels, implicitly, that her father deserves a wide and ample space of his own, suitable to her childish image of him as so much bigger than life. Yet she has no way of giving him that space in the realistic and banal burial ground of the poem; and when she therefore turns her father into Agamemnon, in the italicized lines addressed to him, she simply splits the poem in two, conceptually speaking, with one part in the Winthrop cemetery, the other in ancient Greece.

When Plath rewrites *Electra* as *The Colossus,* she jettisons the realistic scene-setting in the graveyard. The figure of the father has been freed by a daring resort to abstraction. No longer a buried corpse, he is now literally what he has always been in his daughter's imagination (stalled in her eighth year): a colossus. And instead of Winthrop or ancient Greece, we see an unspecified landscape by the sea. What we need to ask is how many symbolic changes follow from this leap of imagination into abstraction, and why they are as surprising as they are.

The Colossus

I shall never get you put together entirely,
Pieced, glued, and properly jointed.
Mule-bray, pig-grunt and bawdy cackles
Proceed from your great lips.
It's worse than a barnyard.

Perhaps you consider yourself an oracle,
Mouthpiece of the dead, or of some god or other.
Thirty years now I have labored
To dredge the silt from your throat.
I am none the wiser.

Scaling little ladders with gluepots and pails of Lysol
I crawl like an ant in mourning
Over the weedy acres of your brow
To mend the immense skull-plates and clear
The bald, white tumuli of your eyes.

A blue sky out of the Oresteia
Arches above us. O father, all by yourself
You are pithy and historical as the Roman Forum.
I open my lunch on a hill of black cypress.
Your fluted bones and acanthine hair are littered

In their old anarchy to the horizon-line.
It would take more than a lightning-stroke
To create such a ruin.
Nights, I squat in the cornucopia
Of your left ear, out of the wind,

Counting the red stars and those of plum-color.
The sun rises under the pillar of your tongue.

My hours are married to shadow.
No longer do I listen for the scrape of a keel
On the blank stones of the landing.
    (*CP,* 129)

The décor of this poem is much reduced from that of *Electra on Azalea Path,* as Plath abstracts the confessional narrative of *Electra* into an anonymous narrative of a single repetitive and reparatory ritual exacted by a symbolic duty. Plath presents us with the broken fragments of a colossus: did she know Henry Moore's statues which disarticulate the heroic recumbent figures of the Parthenon? The colossus is set against a sea, a sky, a hill of black cypress, stars, and a shore-landing. In this scene, a daughter performs an unending labor of cleaning and reconstruction. The tone is equivocal and volatile: it is by turns satiric, desolate, impertinent, quiet, and resigned.

Ted Hughes's remarks on *The Colossus* begin with an account of Plath's experience of the Ouija board and its presider "Prince Otto," who would not speak to her directly, but sent messages indirectly through "spirits":

When she pressed for a more personal communication, she would be told that Prince Otto could not speak to her directly, because he was under orders from The Colossus. And when she pressed for an audience with The Colossus, they would say he was inaccessible. It is easy to see how her effort to come to terms with the meaning this Colossus held for her, in her poetry, became more and more central as the years passed. . . . Late in 1959 . . . she had a dream, which at the time made a visionary impact on her, in which she was trying to reassemble a giant, shattered, stone Colossus. In the light of her private mythology, we can see this dream was momentous, and she versified it, addressing the ruins as "Father," in a poem which she regarded, at the time, as a breakthrough.[9]

We might say that once Plath was able to dream of her father as an immobile set of bleached parts, she had certainly ceased to think of him as a living man, or even as a buried (and still integral) body. The "abstraction" of the poem (and of the dream begetting it) thus stands for the passage of the poet's imagination from the real to the symbolic order. It was a "breakthrough" for Plath—to use her term or Hughes's—to understand that the symbolic order was the correct place to treat the real.

When we compare the form of *The Colossus* to that of *Electra,* we see that rhyme has disappeared. The ceremonious pentameter is gone. The six stanzas are of the same size (five lines each), but the meter is irregular. Suddenly, one is reading the person who became "Plath." But what is it in the style that causes that feeling? Oddly enough, it is first of all the ear's sense of lines ending in a weak syllable: four out of five lines in both the first and second stanzas end this way, establishing a strong presumption that more weak endings are to come (as in fact they are: of the thirty lines of the poem, nineteen—almost two-thirds—end on a weak syllable). Where is this persistent rhythm coming from?[10] (Though *Electra* treats the same theme as *The Colossus,* only six of its forty-six lines end with a weak syllable.) I believe that four obsessive words—*Electra* (subliminally), and *Colossus, Oresteia,* and *father* (visibly present in the poem)—lingered in Plath's preternatural ear, and gave their falling rhythm to *The Colossus.* Aside from the end-words of falling rhythm, other trochaic and dactylic words abound in the poem:[11] such recurrence of a persistent falling rhythm makes up for the absence in the poem of rhyme and of metrically regular lines. Of the eleven end-words in the poem that contradict this falling rhythm by concluding with a strong accent, six (all modified by "your") belong insistently to the Colossus: *your great lips, your throat, your brow, your eyes, yourself, your tongue.* (*Clear, horizon-line, stroke, wind,* and *keel* are the other strong end-words.) Yet at first reading none of this technical skill in rhythm makes itself obvious: Plath's mature poems don't obtrude their technique as the strenuously "polished" juvenilia poems do. Instead, the technique works secretly and powerfully.

If there is no advancing narrative in *The Colossus*—since the point of this static poem is that the daughter's task will never be finished, that nothing will change—what does Plath use instead of plot to bind one part of her poem to another? Instead of constructing a linear story, the poet has arranged a grammatical alternation in which the seesaw of the subject-position pronouns "I" and "you" (or their adjectival form) gives an antiphonal rhythm to the poem. In the following schema I have italicized the subject-pronouns, and have indented, bracketed, and italicized the moments that *don't* belong to the pronominal antiphonal pattern:

> *I* shall never get you put together entirely;
> Perhaps *you* consider *yourself* an oracle;
> Thirty years now *I* have labored; *I* am none the wiser; *I* crawl
>   [*A blue sky arches above us*]
> O father, . . . *you* are pithy and historical.
> *I* open *my* lunch.
> *Your* fluted bones . . . are littered . . .
>   [*It would take more than a lightning stroke*]
> *I* squat in the cornucopia;
>   [*The sun rises under the pillar of your tongue*]
> *My* hours are married to shadow
> No longer do *I* listen.

Plath has built her poem in the form of an arch, in which the pronominal antiphony in the subject-position rises to, and declines from, a central non-pronominal keystone, the "hingeing" middle statement (occupying lines 16–17 in the 30-line poem). Here, the grammatical subject is neither "I" nor "you" but the supervening sky: "A blue sky out of the Oresteia / Arches above us." This keystone contains the only plural pronoun in the poem, the "married" pronoun "us." (Later, when Plath says her hours are married to shadow, the paternal "you" of the "us" has faded into its true spectral state, leaving the "I" solitary once again. The pathos of the central "us" is intensely heightened by that subsequent fading.) In addition to its "keystone" line, *The Colossus* contains two further "objective" statements, both of which also concern the sky: "It would take more than a lightning-stroke / To create such a ruin," and "The sun rises under the pillar of your tongue." These three "objective" sentences, because they lack the pronominal subject-positions "I" and "you" which constitute the rest of the poem, take on oracular and independent force; they belong to fate more than to personal existence.

What can it mean to say, "It would take more than a lightning-stroke / To create such a ruin"? Lightning-strokes are the thunder-bolts of Zeus; Plath seems to imply that above the gods there is a mystery wielding destructive powers which exceed even those of Olympus. Just as the Colossus is colossal, so the Fate that toppled him possesses greater lethal force than the divinities of the *Oresteia*. The grandeur of the father's marble simulacrum, the greatness of his tragic ruin, combine to reduce his enslaved daughter to the size of an ant, as Plath extends the visual scale of the poem's dimensions from the gigantic to the minuscule.

I've been discussing the poem as if it were a conventional elegy arranged around the figure of the Colossus. And so it is, to some degree, but as an elegy it displays many unsettling qualities, among them the vulgarity and comedy that it harbors at its beginning. The housekeeperly expostulation with which the "I" of the poem opens her side of the antiphonal picture, "I shall never get you put together entirely . . . / properly jointed," is matched by the first cacophonous animal "utterances" of the Colossus, as she reports them: "Mule-bray, pig-grunt and bawdy cackles / Proceed from your great lips." *Electra on Azalea Path* could not possibly have admitted such language. The vulgarity comes from Yeats *(Solomon and the Witch),*[12] but it has acquired a Plathian impertinence, which continues in the mocking dismissal ("It's worse than a barnyard") of utterances that would have been, in a conventionally "serious" elegy, the sacred posthumous words of the father.[13] The barnyard element fades as *The Colossus* continues, but the impertinence lingers even after we pass the central keystone: "O father, all by yourself / You are pithy and historical as the Roman Forum."

Of course, the impertinent wit is Plath's authorial defense against the demands of filial piety. She wants so badly to believe her father to be an oracle or a god that she must give over to him the role of pronouncing such a self-definition: "Perhaps you consider yourself an oracle, / Mouthpiece of the dead, or of some god or other." For herself, she will keep her distance, mocking indifferently whatever source of ventriloquism he might proffer. The deliberate domestic details (the "pails of Lysol," the daughter's "lunch") reductively present the archaeological conservation of the Colossus as a tedious task rather than as a sacred trust.

What has become of *Electra on Azalea Plath,* we now ask, as we step back for a moment from our focus on *The Colossus?* Plath has in the second poem recalled, from her first responses at the cemetery, her macabre wish to exhume her father's body, wondering what bodily corruption she would find after twenty years. "My temptation to dig him up. . . . How far gone would he be?" Her imagination now takes her one step beyond that Poe-like fantasy, freeing her into a more positive symbolic act—the re-articulation of the *disjecta membra* of a ruined statue. She blends the wish to re-articulate the corpse with the wish to free her father from the insult of being huddled hugger-mugger with the other dead; and her imagination then creates the disarticulated and isolated marble figure, the undecaying colossus, outstretched in ruin under a pitiless sky, defeating the best efforts of archaeological repair. Plath's piety at the cemetery, as she played a mourning Electra, had resulted in the stifling of one aspect—the furious one—of the psychic energy mobilized in her by the dead father. Now, while describing his archaic grandeur (the tumuli that are his eyes, the acres of his brow), Plath allows her anger at his quasi-suicide—the act of abandonment which makes him incomprehensible to her—to have its say, if only in comic form. Because (being dead) he will not speak to her in English, intelligibly, the animal noises he emits demand translation into her language, just as his disarticulated pieces implicitly demand to be restored to integrity by his daughter's labors.

Yet, even when we have recognized the alternation of grandeur and mockery, even when we perceive the antiphonal structure of first- and second-person pronouns anchored by the remote objectivity of the sky, even when we admit the sentences that seem protected from irony ("Thirty years now I have labored / To dredge the silt from your throat")[14] there are phrases—the best in the poem—that resist our labels. These are groups of words that tersely create a dense complex of feeling. "I crawl like an ant in mourning" can serve as an example of such phrases. Those mere seven words present a complicated feeling composed of several emotional strands: resentment of unjust or at least interminable labor; personal diminution through comparison with the Colossus; a helpless present-tense acknowledgment of inescapable ritual; grief prolonged into minute restitutive reconstruction. Such a combination of sentiments is incapable of any brief definition except a poetic one. Plath has by now learned the art of compression, which is accomplished not by a "forced and rhetorical" Lowellesque crowding of many words together into a dense congestion, but by her own lucid reductions.

Another such intricate feeling-gestalt occurs in the lines,

> Nights, I squat in the cornucopia
> Of your left ear, out of the wind,
>
> Counting the red stars and those of plum-color.

The adverbial "Nights" evokes the habitual cycle of waking and sleeping of the laborer; "I squat" exposes the diminished self, regressed to the primitive habits of a body far from any civilization; "in the cornucopia of your left ear" articulates the infinite resource to be discovered in any single part of the Colossus (not to speak of the whole), but also suggests the daughter's desire to be heard by the father; "out of the wind" reveals the daily insults of the elements, to which the daughter is exposed with no shelter as she clambers over the fragments of her marble father. But the last line of the image-complex, in which the daughter is relieved of her daytime fixation on the marble ruin, represents another dimension entirely. This is the second of the three "aesthetic" moments of the poem: the daughter, freed momentarily from her incessant labors, is at leisure to spend the night "Counting the red stars and those of plum-color." She numbers the stars and relishes their different colors, finding in the very sky whose lightning-bolts symbolize implacable Fate, and whose sun announces exhausting day-labor, a momentary release from filial tragedy.

Plath's best effects, as in these two examples (the ant in mourning and the aesthetic star-count), are produced by a close-worked verbal gestalt which is convincing without being immediately interpretable. Such feeling-clusters are ultimately intelligible because Plath's insistence on clarity drove her to write nothing that was not intellectually founded. But we are gripped by their startling style, their unpredictable grouping of words, before the functions of their individual components are fully understood.

The Colossus convinces, too, by the gradual emergence within it of the daughter's love of the father. As a heap of separate pieces, as a cacophony of uninterpretable utterances, as a desert of immense skull-plates, as an uncategorizable object as full of layers as the Roman Forum, the father is originally a site of frustration and exhaustion. Something changes, however, after the scene is given emotional intelligibility and coherence by the mention of the *Oresteia* in the keystone-sentence "A blue sky out of the Oresteia / Arches above us." Once tragedy has been substituted for incomprehensible injustice, and once the memory of Greek architecture is summoned by the thought of Greek tragedy, the task of the daughter is relieved by a new perception of the ruin, an aesthetic one. This is the first of the three aesthetic moments of the poem, and it parallels the climactic second one of the star-viewing which I have already mentioned. Here, the daughter no longer sees "bald, white tumuli" but rather "fluted bones and acanthine hair." She still resents being obliged to pick up the pieces, as we know from her mutinous use of the word "littered"; and she still aims to rule the disorder, as we know from her present labeling of it as "anarchy." Nonetheless, the aesthetic orientation opened by the words "fluted" and "acanthine" persists in the poem, not merely in the detached appreciation of the star-colors but also in the quasi-psalmic morning obeisance to the Colossus. Every morning, she recalls, speaking to the paternal statue, "The sun rises under the pillar of your tongue"—as if the Colossus' tongue, earlier the source of grunts and brays, has now become, in this third of the three aesthetic moments, one of the supports of an Apollonian temple. What has enabled this admission of love is not the adoption of the persona of Electra, though that has been a way station to *The Colossus;* rather, it is the subsuming of Plath's filial anguish into the complex dialectic of Greek drama, mingling the satyr-play of barnyard grunts with the tragedy of ritual obligation, and emphasizing the personal integration possible through contemplating Fate from the position of aesthetic detachment mediated to us by Greek tragedy.

One of the consequences of the strict, self-contained, and isometric stanzas of *The Colossus* is that we feel an order of aesthetic completion being elicited from the "anarchy" and "ruin" of the landscape, in spite of the desolation of the ending, in which the daughter waits for a rescuer that never comes. The striking power of the close—"No longer do I listen for the scrape of a keel / On the blank stones of the landing"—derives from many sources in the preceding lines. The onomatopoetic "scrape" brings the keel to the ear even while it is being denied; and we feel, as we read of them, that we have already met the "blank stones" of the landing. The feeling of recognition is so strong in part because we have already encountered so many comparable spondees, but also because we have been storing up anticipatory "blank stones" throughout the poem—the Colossus' "great lips," "acres . . . of brow," "immense skull-plates," and "bald, white tumuli." "Fluted bones" are not far from "blank stones," and the "pillar" of the tongue adds yet another sort of stone. In Plath's best work, some accumulation of effect is always taking place, contributing its silent pressure to the "mysterious" (but explicable) conclusiveness of the close.

Plath has come of age as a poet, then, first of all by casting off the spell of her predecessors—from Dickinson to Dylan Thomas, from Yeats to Lowell—and then by achieving, most notably in *The Colossus,* a style of her own, visible especially in her condensed symbolic complexes, some as short as a single phrase ("an ant in mourning"). She has learned to construct a poem with firmness: in *The Colossus* she does so by means of grammar (her antiphonal pronouns and pronominal adjectives); syntax (her alternation of subjective and objective sentences); stanza shape (neat, isometric, short-lined); and rhythm (the poem's distinctive falling cadence). Above all, she has learned to mingle wit and tragedy, to permit the contrary emotions of anger and love to cross and fuse in a single lyric.

Is there anything wrong with *The Colossus?* Yes, if we measure it against Plath's strongest work, some of the austerely chiseled poems of 1962 and 1963. Against their spareness, *The Colossus* may look melodramatic, with its family doom, its exaggerated contrasts of scale, and its gamut of tones. And yes again, if we measure it, in its strict and resigned formality, against Plath's wildest work: set against *Daddy* and *Lady Lazarus,* it may appear repressed. In those poems, the classical lid still confining the anger in *The Colossus* is lifted, as the distinctly unclassical, neogothic myths of vampirism and self-exhibition liberate the violence of Plath's unleashed imaginings (in which ostentatious vulgarity and barbarism are laced with savage joy). And yes once again, if we compare the symbolic proscenium-abstraction of *The Colossus* with the most "human" of Plath's domestic poems, which reach a different sort of intimacy from the anguished and uncanny intimacy of being "married to shadow."

It is a more human intimacy—the result of Plath's most difficult self-reform—that we find when Plath once again takes up the genre of the elegy two years later. In *Parliament Hill Fields* (*CP,* 152) she retains the direct address used in both *Electra* and *The Colossus,* but this time she is addressing the child she lost in a three-months miscarriage on February 6, 1961. The poet herself commented on the poem when she read it on the BBC:

This poem is a monologue. I imagine the landscape of Parliament Hill Fields in London seen by a person overwhelmed by an emotion so powerful as to color and distort the scenery. The speaker here is caught between the old and the new year, between the grief caused by the loss of a child (miscarriage) and the joy aroused by the knowledge of an older child safe at home. Gradually the first images of blankness and silence give way to images of convalescence and healing as the woman turns, a bit stiffly and with difficulty, from her sense of bereavement to the vital and demanding part of her world which still survives. (*CP*, 290–291)

Plath here stresses two things: the antithetical maternal emotions generating the poem (grief and joy); and the gradual evolution of the first ("images of blankness and silence") into the second ("images of convalescence and healing"). That is, she wants to make a poem that, like *The Colossus*, contains in one vessel conflicting emotions, changes its feelings as it goes, and operates chiefly through images.[15] She even keeps the five-line stanza of *The Colossus*. All of these resemblances (and others to be mentioned later) legitimize a close comparison of these two elegies, though my ultimate aim is to define the differences between them—chiefly Plath's stubborn effort, in the second, to open up her previously claustrophobic elegiac universe.

Parliament Hill Fields

On this bald hill the new year hones its edge.
Faceless and pale as china
The round sky goes on minding its business.
Your absence is inconspicuous;
Nobody can tell what I lack.

Gulls have threaded the river's mud bed back
To this crest of grass. Inland, they argue,
Settling and stirring like blown paper
Or the hands of an invalid. The wan
Sun manages to strike such tin glints

From the linked ponds that my eyes wince
And brim; the city melts like sugar.
A crocodile of small girls

Knotting and stopping, ill-assorted, in blue uniforms,
Opens to swallow me. I'm a stone, a stick.

One child drops a barrette of pink plastic;
None of them seem to notice.
Their shrill, gravelly gossip's funneled off.
Now silence after silence offers itself.
The wind stops my breath like a bandage.

Southward, over Kentish Town, an ashen smudge
Swaddles roof and tree.
It could be a snowfield or a cloudbank.
I suppose it's pointless to think of you at all.
Already your doll grip lets go.

The tumulus, even at noon, guards its black shadow:
You know me less constant,
Ghost of a leaf, ghost of a bird.
I circle the writhen trees. I am too happy.
These faithful dark-boughed cypresses

Brood, rooted in their heaped losses.
Your cry fades like the cry of a gnat.
I lose sight of you on your blind journey,
While the heath grass glitters and the spindling rivulets
Unspool and spend themselves. My mind runs with them

Pooling in heel-prints, fumbling pebble and stem.
The day empties its images
Like a cup or a room. The moon's crook whitens,
Thin as the skin seaming a scar.
Now, on the nursery wall,

The blue night plants, the little pale blue hill
In your sister's birthday picture start to glow.
The orange pompoms, the Egyptian papyrus
Light up. Each rabbit-eared
Blue shrub behind the glass

Exhales an indigo nimbus,
A sort of cellophane balloon.
The old dregs, the old difficulties take me to wife.
Gulls stiffen to their chill vigil in the drafty half-light;
I enter the lit house.

(*CP*, 152–153)

Parliament Hill Fields is the poem that most foreshadows Plath's extraordinary later work about her children, such as *Nick and the Candlestick, Child,* and *Balloons.* As an elegy spoken by a mother who has lost a child, it emanates a tenderness that Plath was wary of exhibiting to adults. On the other hand, the speaker of the poem is in some way glad, relieved, that she will not have to bear this child. There are two central statements in the poem, occurring halfway through (in stanzas 5 and 6), together creating a "keystone" strictly comparable to the keystone of *The Colossus.* The first, full of regret, is "Already your doll grip lets go." The second, its contrary, is "I am too happy." The speaker, feeling that her relief is a betrayal of the child, bitterly judges herself to be unlike the "faithful dark-boughed cypresses / [that] Brood, rooted in their heaped losses" and the tumulus that never relinquishes, not even at noon, its "black shadow."

Parliament Hill Fields resembles *The Colossus* not only in adopting its five-line stanza (with ten stanzas instead of six) but also in borrowing its rhythms, using *The Colossus*'s technique of ending lines on weak syllables. Of the fifty lines of *Parliament Hill Fields,* twenty-one (almost half) end in this way. Central words from *The Colossus*—*bald; sun; stone; wind; tumulus; shadow; cypress; blind; image; white; blue; old*—return to remind us that Plath is re-ordering here many of the obsessional counters of the earlier elegy. Plath had not used end-rhymes in *The Colossus,* and *Parliament Hill Fields* seems at first to be an unrhymed poem as well; but Plath decides to make the last line of each stanza rhyme with the first line of the next—an unobtrusive rhyme-pattern that is not noticeable, perhaps, on first reading, but one that, in linking the ten stanzas, makes their sequence feel "meant" rather than arbitrary, a technique unnecessary in a poem as short, repetitive, single-minded, and syntactically and pronominally ordered as the six-stanza *Colossus.*

The two poems are closest in their means of resolution. Two very different moments, we recall, are ensconced in the closing stanza of *The Colossus:* the first is the aesthetic moment of nightly leisure, of numbering the stars and noting their several colors; the second is the moment of flat knowledge of the unrescued future. The closing two stanzas of *Parliament Hill Fields* embrace two exactly comparable moments: the aesthetic moment (in which the fluorescent elements in a picture in the nursery to which the lost child was destined, and in which a living child sleeps, begin to glow in the dark like the stars of *The Colossus);* and the desolate moment when—all farewells to the dead child having been said, the possibilities awakened by its conception put aside—the speaker returns to a flat acknowledgment of "the old dregs, the old difficulties" of her life. Here, for convenience of reference, I reproduce Plath's two closing stanzas:

> Now, on the nursery wall,
>
> The blue night plants, the little pale blue hill
> In your sister's birthday picture start to glow.
> The orange pompoms, the Egyptian papyrus
> Light up. Each rabbit-eared
> Blue shrub behind the glass
>
> Exhales an indigo nimbus,
> A sort of cellophane balloon.
> The old dregs, the old difficulties take me to wife.
> Gulls stiffen to their chill vigil in the drafty half-light;
> I enter the lit house.

Alike though the conclusions of the two poems are (the aesthetic moment followed by the "flat" moment), we notice that Plath has here moved the locus of the aesthetic from the inhuman stars to the human domain of parental love (to the "birthday picture" given to her elder, living child); and she has moved the "flat" moment from solitude (on the ship-landing) to marriage ("take me to wife"). Both of these changes—as well as the replacing of an archaic symbolic landscape by a realistic one—render this poem more approachable and less hieratic than *The Colossus*. The choice of realism here isn't melodramatic and claustrophobic, as it was in the cemetery of *Electra on Azalea Plath*. Rather, Plath is attempting a wider focus, opening her realism to other, objective presences. It was the "objective" use of distant archetypes—sky and sun—in *The Colossus* which enabled this new objectivity in the landscape of the real.

Though I wished to establish first the resemblances between *The Colossus* and *Parliament Hill Fields,* I am more interested in their differences, starting with the non-authorial "objective" beings—gulls and schoolgirls—that turn up in the second poem. The first "extra" characters in the resolution of *Parliament Hill Fields*—of a sort not present in *Electra* or *The Colossus*—are the gulls, who, in the bleak assonance of the close, "stiffen to their chill vigil in the drafty half-light," prolonging the elegiac vigil that the emptied mother has been keeping in memory of the lost child. What are the gulls doing in the poem? They serve as surrogate-spectators, making us aware that no such spectators exist in *Electra* or *The Colossus*. Cosmic presences—here, sky and moon—appear as watchers in *Parliament Hill Fields* as they did in *The Colossus,* but these remote presiders are now joined by local spectators—not only the gulls, but a cluster of schoolgirls. The gulls, serving as intermediaries between the speaker and the landscape, assume, at the close, the burden of her wish to prolong the vigil for the dead child, and also, in their initial appearance, convey—in one of Plath's vivid image-complexes—the speaker's inner conflict, the vexed creating of the poem, and the illness of miscarriage as they "argue, / Settling and stirring like blown paper / Or the hands of an invalid."

The schoolgirls are an "objective" intervention less well-realized than the gulls. Their six lines seem an interruption in the poem, and their obliterative relation to the speaker is exaggerated (their "crocodile," or line, is literalized by Plath as it opens to swallow the speaker). The detail of the "barrette of pink plastic," dropped unnoticed, may be intended as a parallel to the "inconspicuous" lost fetus, but if so, the image is too remote and inanimate to strike home. The schoolchildren may be intimations of the potential child whom the speaker will now never know; but the analogy is not confirmed within the poem. Still, one can see that Plath is resolutely introducing not only animate intermediaries such as the gulls between herself and the indifferent universe, but also human mediators in the form of the schoolgirls. She is working to open up her poetic imagination to the animate and social world, and will do so repeatedly in the future—not always with success, but with a stubborn effort.

The speaker of *Parliament Hill Fields* initially consoles herself, in a conventional elegiac turn, by addressing the vanished person as "you." This ancient means of creating the fiction of continued life is kept afloat by Plath as far as the penultimate stanza of the poem. Here are the lines addressed to the lost infant-to-be: it is noticeable that they creep nearer and nearer to the opening of the stanzas in which they occur:

> Your absence is inconspicuous;
> Nobody can tell what I lack. (st. 1, ll. 4–5)
>
> I suppose it's pointless to think of you at all.
> Already your doll grip lets go. (st. 5, ll. 4–5)
>
> You know me less constant,
> Ghost of a leaf, ghost of a bird. (st. 6, ll. 2–3)
>
> Your cry fades like the cry of a gnat.
> I lose sight of you on your blind journey. (st. 7, ll. 2–3
>
> . . . your sister's birthday picture. (st. 9, l. 2)

Plath's placing of these references to the lost child makes them "fade" into earlier and earlier positions in the stanza, until finally, in the very last stanza, the baby—who has been artificially "kept alive" by the mother's address—disappears altogether into nature, where only gulls keep vigil. No such relinquishment of the object of mourning was allowed to occur in *Electra* or *The Colossus,* where even in the closing stanza ("You died like any man"; "The sun rises under the pillar of your tongue") the father is still being kept alive by being addressed.

But it is not only by such structural means that the baby is made to vanish. The motif of obliteration becomes more and more powerful as the poem proceeds. The sky is "faceless"; the crocodile opens to "swallow" the speaker; the barrette is lost without anyone's noticing; "silence after silence offers itself"; roof and tree are "swaddle[d]" in "an ashen smudge"; the tumulus is shadowed; the dwindling child is addressed, disappearing, as "ghost of a leaf, ghost of a bird." The motif is given its greatest energy when the literal flow of miscarriage, never overtly mentioned, symbolically generates the flow of rivulets in the grass. It is here that Plath's capacity for entwining many emotions in a single complex image, already exemplified in *The Colossus,* powerfully comes into play, as the speaker feels her contact with the child progressively weaken. She strains her sight, but the image fades; she feels the pathos of the undeveloped baby launched on a "blind" journey that it is unequipped to take; the glittering of the heath grass has the steely vivacity of triumphant fate; the spindling rivulets suggest the weakness of the non-viable fetus, dissipating in blood and forgetfulness:

> I lose sight of you on your blind journey,
> While the heath grass glitters and the spindling rivulets
> Unspool and spend themselves. My mind runs with them
>
> Pooling in heel-prints, fumbling pebble and stem.

As the mother tries vainly in imagination to accompany the lost child, her mind strives to follow each rivulet; to her, they call up aspects of the baby on its helpless journey as, not knowing how to live, it does not know how to die; attempting escape, it pools in the false channel of a heel-print; encountering obstacles (a pebble here, a stem there) and not knowing how to cope with them, it "fumbles" its way.

This painfully acquiescent pair of sentences—in which the addressed child is still "alive," even if dissipating in rivulets, and in which Plath (with her customary intuitive use of sound-links) has fused anxiety, grief, resentment of fate, tenderness, and fear—is followed by a single flat epitaph: "The day empties its images / Like a cup or a room." The emptied cup of the womb we know about; and we meet the emptied room two lines later when we glimpse the nursery deprived of its expected inhabitant.

Like *The Colossus, Parliament Hill Fields* takes risks. In the earlier poem, Plath risks inserting into the traditionally grave form of the elegy vulgarity, comedy, and impertinence of tone, combining them with archaic grandeur and aesthetic detachment; in *Parliament Hill Fields* she risks enlarging her earlier claustrophobic elegiac dyad by including the animate gulls and the human schoolgirls. Both poems go beyond the literary derivativeness of *Electra on Azalea Path*. Both have moments of unsettling power as the heat of Plath's imagination compounds many emotions into a single telling verbal complex. As Plath comes of age as a poet, she is prepared, in both *The Colossus* and *Parliament Hill Fields,* to allow more varieties of experience and language (vulgar, quotidian, aesthetic, picturesque, stately, tender, and defeated) to enter the precincts—still strict and stanzaic—of the poem. She has stopped hiding behind the styles of her predecessors, and has become confident in a compressed style of her own, recognizably continuous in imagery and tone with the famous and wrenching poems to come.

It might be argued that I have not met here the most serious criticisms of Plath, the moral ones put forward by such eminent and intelligent critics as Irving Howe and Calvin Bedient. Irving Howe voiced his objections in the closing paragraphs of his essay "The Plath Celebration: A Partial Dissent":[16]

[The poems] are deficient in plasticity of feeling, the modulation of voice that a poet writing out of a controlled maturity of consciousness can muster. Even the best of Sylvia Plath's poems, as her admirer Stephen Spender admits, "have little principle of beginning or ending, but seem fragments, not so much of one long poem, as of an outpouring which could not stop with the lapsing of the poet's hysteria."

Perhaps the hardest critical question remains. Given the fact that in a few poems Sylvia Plath illustrates an extreme state of existence, one at the very boundary of nonexistence, what illumination—moral, psychological, social—can be provided of either this state or the general human condition by a writer so deeply rooted in the extremity of her plight? Suicide is an eternal possibility of our life and therefore always interesting; but what is the relation between a sensibility so deeply captive to the idea of suicide and the claims and possibilities of human existence in general? That her story is intensely moving, that her talent was notable, that her final breakthrough rouses admiration—of course! Yet in none of the essays devoted to praising Sylvia Plath have I found a coherent statement as to the nature, let alone the value, of her vision. Perhaps it is assumed that to enter the state of mind in which she found herself at the end of her life is its own ground for high valuation; but what will her admirers say to those who reply that precisely this assumption is what needs to be questioned.

This is the objection of a critic more attached to novels than to the lyric. A novel has space to relate the sensibility of its protagonist to "the claims and possibilities of human existence in general"; a lyric is, as Lowell says, a "snapshot," and aims at vividness rather than comprehensiveness. To "illuminate"—morally, psychologically, and socially—"the general human condition" is perhaps the aim of novels; but "the general human condition" is of interest to the lyric only aspectually. The lyric shows how someone was feeling on Tuesday morning, fully aware that on Wednesday morning the person may be feeling very different. Every lyric makes the wager that its reader has at some point experienced, if only by analogy, the feelings that it is expressing. Howe seems to suggest that most of us can't feel along with Plath because we cannot find a relation between her experience and ours: "What is the relation between a sensibility so deeply captive to the idea of suicide and the claims and possibilities of human existence *in general?*" (italics mine). But the lyric avoids "human existence in general"; it presents what Hopkins called inscape, the "thisness" of a person or thing or experience: "It is the forgèd feature finds me; it is the rehearsal / Of own, of abrupt self there so thrusts on, so throngs the ear" *(Henry Purcell)*. If Plath has succeeded in cloning herself on the page, psychically and aesthetically, she has done all that art can ask of her, even if Howe wants more.

"In none of the essays devoted to praising Sylvia Plath," Howe adds, "have I found a coherent statement as to the nature, let alone the value, of her vision." I must, in answer, attempt to say briefly what I think the nature of her unsparing vision is, and what value may be found in it. A writer's true "vision" lies in the implications of his or her style. Plath's "vision" admires and promotes anything in language and myth that is able to contain—without denying the existence of—disorder, anarchy, and violence. So the striptease in *Lady Lazarus,* as a measured and willed ritual of exhibition, stylizes the horror of a body that feels itself to be both alive and dead at once; so the gothic fantasy of the vampire in *Daddy,* far too literary to be taken as "real," works to contain the hysteria of the psyche abused by the father's desertion. Plath, like Lawrence, hates the "niceness" of bourgeois concealment: "Dame Kindness, she is so nice! / . . . Sugar can cure everything, so Kindness says." Against bourgeois "sugar" Plath sets emotional truth, "the blood jet" of poetry, and adds: "There is no stopping it" (*Kindness,* 269). The style of a poetry representing "the blood jet" would have to exhibit, as part of its repertoire, both the contained pressure of the artery giving the "jet" its spurt and the peril of its "jetting." One can see the speaker's vectored flight into the sun in *Ariel,* where she is both attached to and propelled by the figure of the horse, as the stylistic embodiment of this component of Plath's "vision."

When critics ask for a writer's "vision," they generally mean a "redemptive vision"—something that answers the question, "Given all we see of meaningless bad luck, physical suffering and death; and given all we know of moral evil, dissimulation, and betrayal, what is there to be said for life?" The demand that a writer have not merely a vision but a "positive" vision seems to me unjust; it ought to be enough that a writer possesses a convincing sense of contemporary existence (no matter how dark) and can bring it unmistakably to life. Plath was not the first to feel that the most rational reaction to "the human condition" is suicide: "Not to be born is the best of all." Perhaps what Plath has to offer her readers is that rarely-spoken Sophoclean truth. As Calvin Bedient brilliantly said of her poetic, "It is the aggressive poetic of one buried alive but not ready to die."[17]

On the moral plane, however, Bedient agrees with Howe:

Her quest [for recognition by, and love from, the father] was by definition immature. And, except as the mote that provoked the splendid blindness of her poetry, what is its importance? Critics maunder about her vision, but as Irving Howe suggests, she had none. She saw neither the next world nor this one. . . . Her sensibility . . . was self-consumed in contradiction. Ambivalence afflicted her.

Bedient continues his criticism of Plath by saying that "the fate of being intended for death, 'perfected' in death alone, lies outside reason and makes us doubt. Far from being a tragedy of will, like classical tragedy, Plath's is a tragedy of weakness, of a fatal vulnerability to the sense of injury" (14). Of course if one considers suicide "a tragedy of weakness," then many notable writers have been "weak," from Chatterton to Celan. But a life-choice (even assuming that the act of suicide is a "choice" rather than a compulsion) is not the same thing as a poem. A poem is always a manifestation of living, even when its subject is death.

Bedient has cited Plath's final and famous poem, *Edge*, to buttress his critique. Let us see what this late elegy, so much the fulfillment of Plath's coming of age as a poet, tells us, and whether its "vision," as Bedient would have us think, "lies outside reason and makes us doubt":

Edge

The woman is perfected.
Her dead

Body wears the smile of accomplishment,
The illusion of a Greek necessity

Flows in the scrolls of her toga,
Her bare

Feet seem to be saying:
We have come so far, it is over.

Each dead child coiled, a white serpent,
One at each little

Pitcher of milk, now empty.
She has folded

Them back into her body as petals
Of a rose close when the garden

Stiffens and odors bleed
From the sweet, deep throats of the night flower.

The moon has nothing to be sad about,
Staring from her hood of bone.

She is used to this sort of thing.
Her blacks crackle and drag.
(*CP*, 272)

Edge (its title at first gnomic) is narrated by an anonymous specta-
tor who describes the corpses of a woman and her two dead children.
They are at first externally observed, but then evoked with an insight
into the woman's motives and her past that only she herself could
possess. So we take the narrating spectator to be the woman herself,
imagining how she would describe the scene if she could view it after
her suicide and infanticide. Throughout the poem, the description is

145

an innately contrastive one: behind the dead woman lies the woman as she was in life. If she is now "perfected," then in life she was "imperfect"; if her dead body now wears the smile of accomplishment, in life it wore the tragic mask of incapacity; if her toga now gives the illusion of being perfectly arranged ("necessary"), in life it was waywardly and unintelligibly arranged. If her bare feet are relieved to "have come so far" on their now-ended journey, in life they were footsore and weary with anxiety. If the children resemble Cleopatra's consoling asps, they have assisted in the only possible escape (as Shakespeare's queen saw it) from future shame and humiliation before the public. If the breasts are now empty of milk, they used to be full, as if lactation (representing the hourly physical demands on a mother) could stop only in death. The poem, in short, is not so much the tale of a life "perfected" in death as the tale of a life that was imperfect, frustrated, unintelligible, weary, already humiliated (the father of the children is absent), spent by the demands of child-rearing, and facing probable further humiliation (in life, Plath faced hospitalization for "insanity" once more). Rather than adopt the mode of complaint (for which Bedient reproaches her—"a fatal vulnerability to the sense of injury") Plath here adopts the stoic reverse of the tone of self-pity. *Edge* is a poem in which Plath is fully aware of her "injuries" but refuses to rail against them as she once had in *Daddy* or *Lady Lazarus*. Contemplating them as ended, in a thought-experiment, she makes them differently visible.

When it begins to recollect the past, *Edge* changes its tone. It is night, and the rose that delighted the day has closed its petals as the garden "stiffens" in rigor mortis. The night flowers can produce their fragrances only by letting them bleed from their seductive "sweet, deep throats."[18] The mother synchronizes her actions with those of nature, folding her children back into her body as the petals of the rose close. This euphemizing of the children's death in intensive vowels *(folded, rose, close; bleed, sweet, deep)* marks the surviving protective tenderness of the mother, as she saves each child from becoming a "bleeding" night-flower like herself. The posthumous voice speaking the poem retains this tenderness, even after death.

We are to infer from *Edge* nothing about the desirability of the murder of the children; rather, by a back-formation of the sort that we practiced in the earlier part of the poem, we are to intuit the gentle living garden of the past, its rose-children with their soft petals. And we are to feel the sadness of the garden's extinction, as it bleeds out its colors and its fragrances. Before she allows the poem to end in pathos, Plath, too, "stiffens," admitting the indifference of the natural universe (in the person of the skeletal moon) to human pain. We are meant to be repelled by the moon "staring from her hood of bone." Her chilling and hardened pragmatism—"She is used to this sort of thing"—precisely tells us that such was not the case in the sensibility of the dead woman. Plath's closure—"Her blacks crackle and drag"—may owe something to Baudelaire's *Recueillement:* the fact of final acquiescence in blackness is very much the same, but where Plath's final tone is harsh, Baudelaire's is gentle:

> Sois sage, O ma Douleur, et tiens-toi plus tranquille.
> Tu réclamais le Soir; il descend; le voici;
> Une atmosphère obscure enveloppe la ville,
> Aux uns portant la paix, aux autres le souci.
>
>   Pendant que des mortels la multitude vile,
> Sous le fouet du Plaisir, ce bourreau sans merci,
> Va cueillir des remords dans la fête servile,
> Ma Douleur, donne-moi la main; viens par ici,
>
>   Loin d'eux. Vois se pencher les défuntes Années
> Sur les balcons du ciel, en robes surannées,
> Surgir du fond des eaux le Regret souriant;
>
>   Le Soleil moribond s'endormir sous un arche;
> Et, comme un long linceul traînant à l'Orient,
> Entends, ma chère, entends, la douce Nuit qui marche.[19]

If one cannot accept Baudelaire's "vision" of a life that offers—to the weary soul full of sorrow over its dead years, grieving its dying sun—only a final rest in Night's trailing shroud, then one can't accept *Edge* either. Knowing the callousness of the "long" moon-perspective that says grimly, "Everyone dies eventually; and what does one life matter?" Plath defends, against the malign moon, the remembered bloom of the rose-garden and its petal-children, even though she must admit, too, the seductive release of the night flower's sweetness as the garden stiffens and bleeds. Under the fictive surface of perfected "Greek necessity" and its "smile of accomplishment," Plath's poem reveals an underimage of life's sorrows, wounds, and humiliations. Refusing the illusion of a future life, the speaker allows her white toga and her white serpent-children the fate of being enwrapped in the stiff crackling and the heavy dragging of an eternal black shroud.

Edge had begun with a pattern of diastole and systole: the line expands, then visibly and strongly contracts, following seven syllables with two. This pattern of contraction is repeated (in stanzas 3, 5, and 6), but in other stanzas the lines resemble each other in length (2, 7–10). The early clipped stanzas, with their scythe-like stanza-ends cutting a sentence in two, are replaced in stanzas 7 and 8 by the wider recollective lines and gentler enjambments symbolic of the garden, past and present; and finally the whole process is brought to a halt by the end-stopped, distanced, icy stanzas of the deathly moon. What is the "vision" of such a poem? It is a vision of a life composed mostly of suffering, but containing within it maternal and sensuous and aesthetic joy of a high order; a vision of the relief offered to mortal "bleeding" by the reversing and projective powers of the imagination; a defense—against the telescopic view which sees human life as paltry—of the poet's close-focus view that can look deep into the throats of the night flowers. Is such a vision one to be repudiated? Or are we glad that it has been articulated so finely, so sorrowfully, in a hundred or so words?

The four elegies I have looked at offer a compact overview of the derivative and imitative Plath *(Electra),* the Plath who has come of age as a poet in both the symbolic and the technical order *(The Colossus),* the adult Plath striving to open the elegy to the wider animate and human world *(Parliament Hill Fields),* and the late Plath who reverts, in her self-elegy, *Edge,* to the Greek dyadic scheme of

The Colossus. But the elegiac dyad has been translated from the paternal generation to the younger one: it is no longer composed of daughter and father, but rather of mother and children. The foretold "edge" is that of the keen knife of self-destruction.

The imagined tableau of *Edge*—one of aesthetic perfection—specifically denies, in its second line, that such bleak tomb-sculpture can ever be compatible with life. By embodying the living children and herself as flowers, directly in the heart of the poem, Plath sets the heartbreaking sensual beauty of flesh and blood in the garden in permanent contradiction to the immobile and sepulchral perfection of the dead. This, surely, is a vision that is authentic, irrefutable, and humanly true.

Appendix: Early Poems by Plath Treating the Father's Death

To show how much work preceded both *Electra on Azalea Plath* and *The Colossus,* I list the titles and initial page-references of earlier poems in the "Juvenilia" and the *Collected Poems* that treat the father's death either entirely or in part:

Sonnet: To Eva (304): The female protagonist is here the fragmented colossus, but the task of reassembling the pieces is identical to that of *The Colossus:* "Not man nor demigod could put together / The scraps of rusted reverie . . ."

Lament: A Villanelle (315): "The sting of bees took away my father / who scorned the tick of the falling weather." Plath commented on this poem (imitative of Dylan Thomas) in her journal: "My villanelle was to my father; and the best one." *The Journals of Sylvia Plath* (New York: Dial Press, 1982), 128.

The Dead (320): "They loll forever in colossal sleep." (The poem has debts to Wordsworth's *A Slumber did my Spirit Seal.*)

Song for a Revolutionary Love (322): "Chuck the broken acropolis out, / fling the seven wonders after that / with struts and props of the holy stage."

Touch-and-Go (335): "On this same fugue, unmoved, / Those stonier eyes look / Safe-socketed in rock."

Conversation Among the Ruins (21): Though this poem seems to be about an unsuccessful love-affair, the landscape is that of *The Colossus:* "Fractured pillars frame prospects of rock; . . . I sit / Composed in Grecian tunic and psyche-knot, / . . . the play turned tragic."

Letter to a Purist (36): A love-poem that opposes the lover to "That grandiose colossus who / Stood astride / The envious assaults of sea."

Spider (48): This is the source of the poet's self-image in *The Colossus* as "an ant in mourning." The spider traps an ant, and yet another: still,

> The ants—a file of comers, a file of goers—
> Persevered on a set course
> No scruple could disrupt,
> Obeying orders of instinct till swept
> Off-stage and infamously wrapped
> Up by a spry black deus
> Ex machina. Nor did they seem deterred by this.

The passage has relevance to Plath's repeated suicide attempts, which recur without her volition, instinctively: even after "the spry black deus / Ex machina" has "swept [her] off-stage" and "wrapped [her] up," she persists in "obeying orders of instinct," "not deterred" by previous experience.

Two Views of Withens (71): A comparison is made between the unlucky speaker who finds "bare moor, / A colorless weather, / And the House of Eros / Low-lintelled, no palace," and a luckier correspondent (unidentified) who has sent a letter presumably from Greece: "You, luckier, / Report white pillars, a blue sky, / The ghosts, kindly."

Ouija (77): Although the poem seems to concern Plath's relation with Hughes, as she and he invoke the Ouija board together, the presiding spirit is a god who "Rises to the glass from his black fathoms." As Hughes reports, "Her father's name was Otto, and 'spirits' would regularly arrive with instructions for her from one Prince Otto, who was said to be a great power in the underworld." Ted Hughes, "Sylvia Plath and Her Journals," in Paul Alexander, ed.,

Ariel Ascending: Writings about Sylvia Plath (New York: Harper & Row, 1985), 155.

On the Decline of Oracles (78): "My father died . . . But I, I keep the voices he / Set in my ear, and in my eye / The sight of those blue, unseen waves."

Perseus: The Triumph of Wit Over Suffering (82): The poem is addressed to Perseus, the personification of "Wit" and comedy. The argument says that "the mammoth, lumbering statuary of sorrow" can only be digested by "a bigger belly / Still than [the one that] swallows joy," to wit, the "cosmic / Laugh" of Perseus, who holds in his hand a scales, "the celestial balance / Which weighs our madness with our sanity." "Madness" has resulted from the speaker's inability to digest rock:

> the whole globe
> Expressive of grief turns gods, like kings, to rocks.
> Those rocks, cleft and worn, themselves then grow
> Ponderous and extend despair on earth's
> Dark face.

In the presence of comedy and wit, tragedy dissolves, and Plath utters its epitaph:

> Where are
> The classic limbs of stubborn Antigone?
> The red, royal robes of Phèdre? the tear-dazzled
> Sorrows of Malfi's gentle duchess?
> Gone.

Sculptor (91): Though ostensibly a tribute to Leonard Baskin, the poem presents the dead begging the sculptor to make effigies of them until "his chisel bequeaths / Them life livelier than ours, / A solider repose than death's." Plath's effort to memorialize her father as sculpted statuary is evident.

Full Fathom Five (92): Otto Plath, as the old man of the sea, is compared to an iceberg and a statue: "the archaic trenched lines / Of your grained face shed time in runnels." "One of my best and most curiously moving poems, about my father-sea god-muse," said Plath, who was considering using it as the title-poem for the book later called *The Colossus* (according to Ted Hughes's Introduction to the *Collected Poems*, 13).

Moonrise (98): Though this is a meditation on Lucina, goddess of the moon and of childbirth, it includes a passage on whiteness as the color of death, which turns water itself into rock:

> White: it is a complexion of the mind.
>
> I tire, imagining white Niagaras
> Build up from a rock root.

And it turns out that Lucina, "bony mother," "drag[s] our ancient father at the heel, / White-bearded, weary."

Child's Park Stones (100): Stones set up by "some founding father" become, in this poem of rhymed *(ababa)* Mooresque syllabics (7-8-9-8-7), figures for the dead:

> No man's crowbar could
> Uproot them: their beards are ever-
> Green. Nor do they, once in a hundred
> Years, go down to drink the river:
> No thirst disturbs a stone's bed.

Poems, Potatoes (106): Assimilates poems to amoral stone: "Stones, without conscience, word and line endure."

A Winter Ship (112): Although beginning with a wharf at which crabs are being unloaded, the poem ends by imagining the sea "farther out," where "the waves will be mouthing icecakes," and it ends: "We wanted to see the sun come up / And are met, instead by this iceribbed ship," the "albatross of frost" recorded in the title of the poem, a recollection of Coleridge's death-ship.

Suicide off Egg Rock (115): A male figure is imagined who has committed suicide. He is (unlike the Colossus), subject to natural decay, "His body beached with the sea's garbage."

All of these poems are sedulously worked.

I F MILTON'S *L'Allegro* shows us a young poet who has pondered how to deal with action and contemplation, the pagan and the Christian (the latter by omission), the baser and higher senses, the ethics of social orders, the hierarchy of aesthetic value, the enumeration of the world's attractions, the extension of joys in time and space, and the management of irreproachable and exquisite iambic tetrameter couplets; if Keats's *On First Looking into Chapman's Homer* shows us a young poet who has learned to make the Petrarchan sonnet both personally authentic and widely shareable, convincing in the logical surprises of its images, inventive in its playing of rhyme-units against syntax, and intellectually daring in epic reach, while being willing to reject, a year later, all he has done in favor of a Shakespearean tragic perspective; if Eliot's *Love Song of J. Alfred Prufrock* shows us a young poet who has succeeded not only in integrating, in one long monologue, multiple discourses embodying both pain and satirical irony, but also in casting them into a seductive rhythmic movement which embraces two lyrics within its narrative; and if Plath's *The Colossus* shows us a young poet who has made the leap from the confessional to the abstract, from the self-pitying to the objectively symbolic, a process she will continue and refine through *Parliament Hill Fields* and *Edge,* then we can begin to appreciate all that any young poet has to master in order to write a poem that will endure. These four writers, all merely in their twenties when they wrote these strikingly original four poems, exemplify experiment as well as learning; an intent understanding of the potential of their medium as well as of the traditions of their genre; a drive toward the authentic representation of their individual temperament; and a love of the conventions within which they could achieve, and against which they could perfect, that representation. As we see new authors coming of age as poets, we will find in them comparable learning, experiment, generic invention, and imaginative mastery.

NOTES

CREDITS

INDEX

Notes

Introduction

1. Helen Darbishire, *The Early Lives of Milton* (New York: Barnes and Noble, 1965), 10.

2. *The Poems of Emily Dickinson: Variorum Edition,* ed. R. W. Franklin, 3 vols. (Cambridge, Mass.: Harvard University Press, 1998). This is poem #790 in Franklin's numbering.

3. Although Eliot and Plath went on to free verse, they, like the other two poets considered here, began by writing formal verse in meter and rhyme, so my remarks presume a beginning of that sort.

4. I will have more to say about unevenness of style with respect both to Keats's first sonnets and to Eliot's canceled version of some verses for *Prufrock,* now printed as *Prufrock's Pervigilium,* in *Inventions of the March Hare: Poems 1909–1917,* ed. Christopher Ricks (London: Faber & Faber, 1996).

1. John Milton: The Elements of Happiness

1. Cleanth Brooks, *The Well-Wrought Urn* (New York: Reynal & Hitchcock, 1947), 48. See the description in *A Variorum Commentary on the Poems of John Milton,* ed. A. S. P. Woodhouse and Douglas Bush (New York: Columbia University Press, 1972), II, 251–252 (hereafter referred to as *Variorum,* II). This commentary and the volumes of *Milton: The Critical Heritage,* ed. John T. Shawcross (London and Boston: Routledge & Kegan Paul, 1972) give a full idea (up to 1972) of commentary on the two poems, which are scarcely ever separated. In flicking back and forth from one poem to the other, critics have failed to give a unified account of *L'Allegro,* always slighted in comparison to *Il Penseroso.* Miltonists, being chiefly interested in the development of Milton's moral and

philosophical being, rather than in the aesthetic completions of a poem in itself, find *L'Allegro* charming but dismiss it as philosophically unserious. Empson dismissed both poems as "ponderous trifles with a few good lines in them" (*Variorum*, II, Part One, 252). The best piece of writing on the two works as poems is G. Wilson Knight, "The Frozen Labyrinth: An Essay on Milton," in *The Burning Oracle* (London, 1939), 59–113. (See the description in *Variorum*, II, 247–248.) Though Knight is critical, and his frame of reference is (perhaps unfairly) the later Milton, he is accurate in saying that the images in these two poems are "pictorially still, a sequential arrangement of tiny solids with no sense of any dynamic, evolving energy. The task of marrying movement and action to design, the realizing of an organic cohesion of motion and solidity, of the melodic and the architectural, remains unattempted: though the arts corresponding to each of these elements *in isolation* are insistently, almost excessively, emphasized" (64). I shall have more to say about these "tiny solids," Milton's lists of elements. Blake's illustrations of the poems show a clear preference for the state to which the protagonist has evolved by *Il Penseroso*, leaving trivial joys behind and becoming a sage. Blake's frivolous *Mirth* is much reduced from Milton's.

2. The texts of both poems are taken from *Poems of Mr. John Milton, Both English and Latin . . . 1645*, as reproduced in *The Riverside Milton*, ed. Roy Flannagan (Boston: Houghton Mifflin, 1998).

3. Because Milton placed the Ode first among the English poems in 1645, and because of the degree to which its themes (like those of *Il Penseroso*) foreshadow the later Milton, many Miltonists have seen the Ode as the first "great" poem, a "masterpiece." See, for example, the *Variorum* passim, and Douglas Bush, *John Milton* (New York: Collier Books, 1967). Milton may have placed it first among the English poems because it instructs him to bring his gift to the Savior; it is in that sense a dedicatory poem. Of course, Milton may, like his commentators, have prized it for its ambition and the centrality to his thinking of its Incarnational theme.

4. The prosody of the Nativity Ode is a subject in itself. The formal description of the ode is as follows: the 4-stanza proem is composed, with allegorical fitness, in rime royal, but with a Spenserian hexameter in the final line; the 27-stanza "Hymn" that follows is composed of 8-line stanzas comprising a sestet and a couplet, rhyming *aabccbdd*. The lines are of the following lengths: 33533546. The non-isometric couplet (a tetrameter coupled with a hexameter) is itself somewhat uneasy.

In both proem and "Hymn," the mid-points of the hexameters (where a caesura is conventionally expected) are sometimes awkwardly placed: "And chose with us a dark- / som House of mortal Clay"; "Was all that did their sil- /

ly thoughts so busie keep"; "The dreadfull Judge in mid- / dle Air shall spread his throne." (Even if one were to place the caesura after the seventh syllable, the consequent separation of adjective and noun makes, in such lines, for an unidiomatic pause: "Was all that did their silly / thoughts so busie keep.")

Initial reversed feet (normally used for accenting a force in image or theme) appear at moments where they are antagonistic to the "soft" or "smooth" effect being described:

> She crown'd with Olive green, came softly sliding
> *Down* through the turning sphear.

> The Windes with wonder whist,
> *Smoothly* the waters kist,
>   *Whispering* new joyes to the milde Ocean.
>   [italics mine]

5. Rosemond Tuve, *Images and Themes in Five Poems by Milton* (Cambridge, Mass.: Harvard University Press, 1957), 22ff.

6. T. S. Eliot, "A Note on the Verse of John Milton," *Essays and Studies* 21 (1936), reprinted as "Milton I," in *On Poetry and Poets* (New York: Farrar, Straus, 1957): "The imagery in *L'Allegro* and *Il Penseroso* is all general. . . . It is not a particular ploughman, milkmaid, and shepherd that Milton sees (as Wordsworth might see them); the sensuous effect of these verses is entirely on the ear, and is joined to the concepts of ploughman, milkmaid, and shepherd."

7. *Variorum*, II, 274.

8. Ibid., 304–305.

9. The same competitiveness appears in lines 22ff. of the ode *On the Morning of Christ's Nativity*, in which Milton wishes to present his own gift of song even before the Magi can arrive at the stable with their offerings:

> See how from far upon the Eastern rode
> The Star-led Wisards haste with odours sweet,
> O run, prevent them with thy humble ode,
> And lay it lowly at his blessèd feet;
> Have thou the honour first, thy Lord to greet.

10. The two editions of the poem differ in line 104: though in its first publication in the *Poems* of 1645 the line reads, as here, "And he by Friars Lanthorn led," in 1673 it reads "And by the Friars Lanthorn led." Modern editors generally have preferred the 1645 reading, which shows a male teller bursting in on the female teller's tale with a tale of his own.

11. Milton's tetrameters have been well analyzed by Edward R. Weismiller in *Variorum*, II, 1026–1036. He covers the arguments of prosodists concerning their character as trochaic or iambic in nature, concluding that since so few lines end in a complete trochee, the meter should be considered fundamentally iambic. The varying placement of the caesura in Milton's tetrameters (a major source of their aural appeal) is beautifully illustrated by Thomas Gray in his "Observations on English Metre," cited in *Milton 1732–1801: The Critical Heritage,* ed. Shawcross, II, 250–251.

12. See, however, Edward R. Weismiller, "Studies of Verse Form in the Minor English Poems," in the *Variorum,* II, Part Three, 1007–1036. Weismiller mentions a few instances of supposedly ambiguous feet on pp. 1027–1028, but they are to my mind not ambiguous.

13. The rapidity with which this sort of syntax can become ridiculous is evident in Joyce Kilmer's *Trees,* an imitation of this part of *L'Allegro:*

> I think that I shall never see
> A poem lovely as a tree,
> A tree that may in summer wear
> A nest of robins in her hair,
> Upon whose bosom snow has lain,
> Who intimately lives with rain [etc.].

14. For a detailed examination of the rhythms of the poem, see Weismiller, "Studies of Verse Form."

2. John Keats: Perfecting the Sonnet

1. Keats's poems are cited and dated from *The Poems of John Keats,* ed. Jack Stillinger (Cambridge, Mass.: Harvard University Press, 1978). Keats's letters are cited and dated from *The Letters of John Keats: 1814–1821,* ed. Hyder Rollins (Cambridge, Mass.: Harvard University Press, 1958), abbreviated in the text as "L," followed by the volume and page number.

2. One piece in Keats's first category, "Poems," is in fact a sequence of three sonnets, and the dedicatory poem to Leigh Hunt, Keats's literary benefactor, is also a sonnet, making 21 sonnets in all. The 17 numbered sonnets in the third group are not arranged in chronological order of composition: Keats set first the sonnet "To My Brother George," as a second, internal, familial dedication: "[W]hat, without the social thought of thee / Would be the wonders of the sky and sea?"

3. Although quatrain and sestet forms were essential to the odes, the Shakespearean couplet, it seems, was not in Keats's mind while composing them (though it may have influenced his invention of the magical retarding couplet-within-the-septet in *To Autumn*).

4. Keats's early practice follows Hunt, whose sonnets are all Petrarchan (though in the essay cited below, Hunt gives examples of other kinds: blank verse sonnets, "tailed" sonnets, Spenserian and Shakespearean sonnets, and so forth). Hunt had written sonnets, imitated by Keats, on Kosciusko, Haydon, and the Nile, among others; and he had played—but only once—with sonnet rhyme (rhyming an entire sonnet, the "Iterating Sonnet," on the single compound word "United States"). See Leigh Hunt, *Poetical Works,* ed. H. S. Milford (London: Oxford University Press, 1923), 235–253. See also Hunt's "Essay on the Cultivation, History, and Varieties of the Species of Poem called the Sonnet" in *The Book of the Sonnet,* ed. Leigh Hunt and S. Adams Lee (Boston: Roberts Brothers, 1867), 3–91.

5. Keats's correction of "low-brow'd" to "deep-brow'd" and his replacement of two vague draft lines by "Yet did I never breathe its pure serene" reflect his capacity for self-criticism even when he is writing a poem far above the level of most of its predecessors.

6. By raising the eyes, rather than the legs, to a given height, Keats can combine sobriety and "wingedness." He achieves the same effect in *To Autumn* when, in the last line, rather than saying that the gathering swallows twitter "from" the skies (thereby placing their spectator below them on the earth receiving their song), he says that they twitter "in" the skies (making the spectator lift his eyes to the place of their twittering).

7. For purposes of comparison, I cite the execrable poem by Hunt:

To the Grasshopper and the Cricket

Green little vaulter in the sunny grass,
    Catching your heart up at the feel of June,
    Sole voice that's heard amidst the lazy noon,
When ev'n the bees lag at the summoning brass;—
And you, warm little housekeeper, who class
    With those who think the candles come too soon,
    Loving the fire, and with your tricksome tune
Nick the glad silent moments as they pass;—
O sweet and tiny cousins, that belong,

One to the fields, the other to the hearth,
Both have your sunshine; both, though small, are strong
 At your clear hearts; and both were sent on earth
To sing in thoughtful ears this natural song—
 In doors and out,—summer and winter,—Mirth.
  (*Poetical Works*, 240)

8. Leigh Hunt had written a sonnet called *The Poets*, in which, asked the desert-island question, he chose Spenser over Shakespeare for solace in sorrow:

But which take with me, could I take but one?
 Shakespeare,—as long as I was unoppressed
  With the world's weight, making sad thoughts intenser;
But did I wish, out of the common sun,
 To lay a wounded heart in leafy rest,
  And dream of things far off and healing,—Spenser.
   (*Poetical Works*, 239)

9. Although there are other sonnets by Keats that end in a hexameter (1, 13, and 57), it is here that the effect most seems to carry thematic meaning.

3. T. S. Eliot: Inventing Prufrock

1. T. S. Eliot, *Inventions of the March Hare: Poems 1909–1917*, ed. Christopher Ricks (London: Faber & Faber, 1996), 83. Subsequent references in the text will be abbreviated as *MH*, followed by the page number. I am much indebted to this edition throughout this chapter.

2. *TLS* (5 April 1928), quoted in *MH*, 392–393.

3. *Poetry* (September 1946), 25; *MH*, 388.

4. "What Dante Means to Me," *To Criticize the Critic* (New York: Farrar, Straus & Giroux, 1965), 390.

5. See *MH*, 39–47, for the version of *Prufrock* containing the *Pervigilium*; for Ricks's magisterial notes on it, see pp. 176–190.

6. Preface to *Poems Written in Early Youth* (New York: Farrar, Straus & Giroux, 1967), 7–8; *MH*, xxxviii.

7. "A Prediction in Regard to Three English Authors," *Vanity Fair* (February 1924); *MH*, 413.

8. The final sentence of this excerpt echoes, unpropitiously but perhaps unconsciously, the end of Browning's *Porphyria's Lover:* "And yet God has not said a word!" We'll soon come to another echo of the same poem.

9. *Varieties of Metaphysical Poetry,* ed. Ronald Schuchard (London: Faber & Faber, 1993), 128, cited in *MH,* 207.

10. See Ricks's elaborate note on "horns," *MH,* 226. I cannot think that horns that "toss and toss" are those of a (stable) altar.

11. From Dante's *Inferno,* Canto 27, ll. 61–66. Guido da Montefeltro consents to reply, after Dante questions him: "If I thought that my reply were to be to someone who would ever return to the world, this flame would be still, without further motion. But since no one has ever returned alive from this depth, if what I hear is true, I answer you without fear of shame." I follow Eliot's spelling of Italian.

12. T. S. Eliot, *Collected Poems* (New York: Harcourt, Brace, 1952), 3–7.

13. Although the rhymes in *Prufrock* are mostly monosyllabic, Eliot takes care to make them interestingly semantically aslant, collocating *hotels* and *shells, drains* and window-*panes, create* and *plate, stair* and *hair, chin* and *pin,* and so on. A naïve poet tends to join like to like. When Eliot does this *(indecisions, revisions)* he makes sure that we know he is doing it—here, by the ostentatious rhyme of a quadrisyllable with a trisyllable).

4. Sylvia Plath: Reconstructing the Colossus

1. Linda Wagner-Martin, in *Sylvia Plath: A Literary Life* (New York: St. Martin's Press, 1999), objects to the label "Juvenilia" attached by Ted Hughes to these poems, commenting, "It is the contention of this study . . . that Plath was a serious writer throughout her college years, beginning in 1950. . . . It seems clear that her poetry should be considered 'mature' long before 1956." In my view, the college years produced poetry that was externally technically accomplished and psychologically truthful, but not yet poetically "mature"—that is, it was not yet a poetry in which "technique" is intrinsic to theme. I therefore retain Hughes's label, "Juvenilia."

2. Sylvia Plath, *Collected Poems,* ed. Ted Hughes (New York: Harper Perennial, 1981), 15. Further citations and dates are drawn from this edition (hereafter *CP*) and will be inserted parenthetically in the text. I follow the convention of the Index of *CP* in giving only the initial page number of the poems cited.

3. This information is taken from Wagner-Martin, *Sylvia Plath,* 4. The author quotes "an unpublished 1968 letter" by Aurelia Plath, Sylvia's mother, de-

scribing "the four years of horrible illness, reactions I kept the children from witnessing" by serving their meals in their upstairs playroom while their father remained in his first-floor "bedroom-study" (11). It can be assumed that Sylvia Plath, between the ages of four and eight, could not have been entirely immune to her father's "reactions," in spite of her mother's efforts.

4. Paul Alexander, in *Rough Magic: A Biography of Sylvia Plath* (New York: Viking, 1991), 135, quotes Philip McCurdy (in an interview) citing a statement made to him by Plath: "When she was ten she slit her throat, she said, and showed him a scar which, whether she invented the story or not, he could plainly see." See also *Lady Lazarus:* "One year in every ten / I manage it . . . // What a trash / To annihilate each decade" (*CP,* 244, 245).

5. Though Plath did not publish this poem in her first book, she thought well enough of it to read it aloud on the BBC in January 1963.

6. The 66-line, 5-stanza *Electra* alternates between two pentameter stanza-forms: stanzas 1, 3, and 5 have ten lines, stanzas 2 and 4 have eight lines. Although the poem has been described as having an undeviating set of rhyme-schemes—one for the ten-line stanzas *(abccdbeeda)* and one for the eight-line stanzas *(abbcddca)*—this is not strictly true: stanza 3 allows an anomaly. The two lines in it which "should" rhyme with each other as *d*-rhymes according to the ten-line scheme (lines 5 and 9) don't. The end-words that don't rhyme with anything else are "you" (line 5) and "dye" (line 9). When we ask ourselves the reason for this anomaly, we discover another constraint that Plath has placed upon herself in composing the poem: each stanza must contain, in some form, the word "die." In stanza 3 (the anomalous stanza) it appears as "dye" (and in stanza 4 as the final syllable of "trage-dy"). The observance of this rule doesn't explain why Plath didn't find a rhyme for "die" to put in the place of "you," unless perhaps she wanted to alert her reader—by the presence of the anomaly—to the "necessary" presence of the root-word "die" throughout.

7. *The Variorum Edition of the Poems of W. B. Yeats,* ed. Peter Allt and Russell K. Alspach (London: Macmillan, 1940; reprinted 1989), 622.

8. As John Frederick Nims remarked, "The rhymes we find in *The Colossus* [the volume] are already at an advanced stage of their evolutionary history. We can assume that hundreds of earlier poems had exhausted, for the time, the poet's taste for full rhyme. . . . By preference she rhymes . . . atonally. The same vowel sound but with different consonants after it. . . . Different vowel sounds but with the same final consonant." "The Poetry of Sylvia Plath: A Technical Analysis," in *Ariel Ascending: Writings about Sylvia Plath,* ed. Paul Alexander (New York: Harper & Row, 1985), 46–60; 51.

9. Ted Hughes, "Sylvia Plath and Her Journals," in *Ariel Ascending*, ed. Alexander, 152–164; 155, 157.

10. Plath had used falling rhythm before: the nearby poem, *Suicide off Egg Rock*, is full of it. But that poem is still in thrall to Lowell, as *The Colossus* so resolutely is not.

11. Some of these words can be scanned as spondees (e.g., *mule-bray, skull-plates*), but in such compound nouns the first component is accented more heavily than the second, and therefore I count such words among those exhibiting trochaic and dactylic form. These are: *properly, mule-bray, pig-grunt, bawdy, mouthpiece, thirty, scaling, little, ladders, gluepots, weedy, acres, skull-plates, tumuli, arches, father, pithy, historical, Roman, fluted, acanthine, anarchy, horizon, lightning, counting, pillar, married.* One is reminded, by Plath's insistence on the falling rhythm of *Electra, father,* and *Oresteia,* of Strauss's powerful use of the same rhythm in the name *Agamemnon* as a motif in his *Elektra.*

12. Who understood
    Whatever has been said, sighed, sung,
    Howled, miau-d, barked, brayed, belled, yelled, cried, crowed,
    Thereon replied. . . .
       Solomon and the Witch (*Variorum Yeats*, 387)

13. In a reading that depends on the child psychology of Winnicott, David Holbrook, in *Sylvia Plath: Poetry and Existence* (London: The Athlone Press, 1988), hazards that the sounds made by the Colossus are adult language as first heard by a child. "All she has are the strange noises of father when she was an infant, and she associates these with puzzling, as she did then, about what he makes of her" (157). Plath does not here represent herself as a child, however; and the source of the unintelligibility of the noises is that the Colossus behaves like "an oracle, / Mouthpiece of the dead, or of some god or other." Oracles are notoriously unintelligible: see Plath's intention (mentioned in the *Journals*) to use a passage from De Chirico as an epigraph to her poem "On the Decline of Oracles": "Inside a ruined temple the broken statue of a god spoke a mysterious language" (*The Journals of Sylvia Plath* [New York: Dial Press, 1982], 211).

14. One may ask why—since Plath is still in her twenties when she composes the poem—she asserts that she has labored at her task of reconstruction for thirty years. The answer is that "Twenty years" would not alliterate with "throat": the lines would lose their "binding secret" (Seamus Heaney) which makes them seem "inevitable" rather than accidental.

15. *Parliament Hill Fields*, perhaps because it is a "quiet" poem, has not

drawn much commentary. My claims for the success of *Parliament Hill Fields* are not admitted by all: Marjorie Perloff, for instance, once judged that the poem "often substitutes contrivance for emotional coherence," and adds that "Lines— or for that matter, whole stanzas—could be reversed without changing the poem appreciably." She found the tone of the poem "too self-indulgent." See "On the Road to *Ariel:* The 'Transitional' Poetry of Sylvia Plath," in *Sylvia Plath: The Woman and the Work,* ed. Edward Butscher (New York: Dodd, Mead, 1977), 125–142; 129, 132–133. Most books on Plath center on the more theatrical poems; I would like to see this quiet poem become better known.

16. In *Sylvia Plath: The Woman and the Work,* ed. Butscher, 225–235; 235.

17. "Sylvia Plath, Romantic," in *Sylvia Plath: New Views on the Poetry,* ed. Gary Lane (Baltimore: Johns Hopkins University Press, 1979), 3–18; 18.

18. Plath generalizes "the night flower" as single, like herself; but by multiplying the "throats" she multiplies and humanizes the flowers in the garden, finding suffering the inevitable condition of both life and art.

19. See *"Les Fleurs du Mal": The Complete Text of "The Flowers of Evil"/ Charles Baudelaire; in a new translation by Richard Howard* (Boston: David R. Godine, 1982). On p. 173 is Howard's translation (reprinted by permission of David R. Godine, Publisher, Inc.; translation copyright ©1982 by Richard Howard):

Meditation

Behave, my Sorrow! let's have no more scenes.
Evening's what you wanted—evening's here:
a gradual darkness overtakes the town,
bringing peace to some, to others pain.

Now, while humanity racks up remorse
in low distractions under Pleasure's lash,
grovelling for a ruthless master—come
away, my Sorrow, leave them! Give me your hand . . .

See how the dear departed dowdy years
crowd the balconies of heaven, leaning down,
while smiling out of the sea appears Regret;

the Sun will die in its sleep beneath a bridge,
and trailing westward like a winding-sheet—
listen, my dear—how softly Night arrives.

Credits

Index